Haunted Inns
of
Kent

Roger Long

S.B. Publications

Also by Roger Long

MURDER IN OLD BERKSHIRE 1990
I'LL BE HANGED 1991
THE CROWTHORNE CHRONICLES 1992 (2002)
HAUNTED INNS OF THE CHILTERNS AND THAMES VALLEY 1993
FINAL COMMITMENT 1994
ANCIENT BERKSHIRE INNS AND THEIR STORIES 1996
HAUNTED INNS OF HAMPSHIRE 1999
CAESAR'S CIRCLE 2000
HAUNTED INNS OF SUSSEX 2001
HAUNTED INNS OF SURREY 2002
CLARISSA'S PIG 2003
GRIM ALMANAC OF OLD BERKSHIRE 2004

First published in 2005 by S. B. Publications
Tel: 01323 893498
Email: sbpublications@tiscali.co.uk

ISBN 1-85770-301-4

Designed and Typeset by EH Graphics (01273) 515527
Printed by Ethos Productions Ltd.

Publisher's Note: Whilst every care has been taken to ensure the accuracy of all the
information contained in this book neither the author nor the publisher can accept
responsibility for any mistakes that may occur.

Illustrations: Brenda Allaway   Compilation: Dave Blackman

Dedicated to Harry Kinch, a gentleman of Kent

Contents

Foreword

Dear Reader,

This is my 14th book and my 6th one on haunted inns. It follows The Chilterns, Berkshire, Hampshire, Sussex and Surrey. My extensive and intensive study has necessitated my visiting 1500 different pubs to find 300 haunted ones, no wonder I have slimmed down to a mere 15 stones.

Kent is the furthest I've been from Royal Berkshire in this ambitious exercise, which in turn has necessitated seven separate nights at various hotels. Bang goes any potential profit on this book.

What does this interloper know of Kent? I hear you asking.

Quite a lot actually.

Many of my formative years were spent with the gypsies and Cockneys 'op pickin' and I spent countless holidays with my wife's relatives at 'Margut'.

Broadstairs is probably the country's most attractive seaside town and I have had so many pub crawls around Gillingham that I look upon some of the watering holes as my locals. I have friends in Chatham, Maidstone, Ramsgate, Westerham and Dover but I make a point of not staying with them because of the scathing looks their wives give me when they can't get up for work the next morning.

Back to the book 'Haunted Inns of Kent' the reader will find some 50 of them. I am a little surprised that at least 20 have not been mentioned before by better-known Kent writers. Why did it take a blue-eyed country Berkshire boy to discover them?

As in all of my books I have visited every site mentioned; the inns that is. In addition some 80 unlicensed sites are also included, albeit briefly. Where these sites can be credited to other authors I have named them and hopefully given them sufficient appreciation and homage.

Enjoy the book.

ROGER LONG

The Castle Inn at Chiddingstone

Chiddingstone, this gem of a Weald village, takes its name from the Chiding Stone. The stone is one of two large boulders found on a small common reached by a footpath, midway down the High Street in the vicinity of the tiny village school. The flat stone is thought to have been the scene of a Druids' judicial court but evidence is pretty tenuous.

Back to the Castle Inn. It lies at the bottom of the High Street's picturesque cluster of Tudor houses. The Inn, along with its neighbours, has been centre stage of numerous film sets over the years. It is owned by the National Trust and has been a hostelry since 1730, but the building is much older. Romantic speculation suggests that the Castle Inn was the place where Anne Boleyn was forced to spend the night when caught in a blizzard on her way to Hever, some two or three miles to the east.

Readers will be relieved to know that Anne Boleyn does not haunt

the Castle Inn. Poor Anne is reputed to be the most overworked ghost in Britain with at least a dozen venues making regular reports of sightings. Good Queen Bess and Dick Turpin however would seem to give her a run for her money. As far as I know the Castle Inn has no internal spectre. But outside, near Chiddingstone Castle's gates, after which the Inn was named, is a favourite haunt of Ann Streatfield. Ann, the daughter of the Earl of Leicester of neighbouring Penshurst, married Henry Streatfield whose family had owned Chiddingstone for generations. The Castle was known as High Street House and was the pride of the Streatfields, who had made a fortune in the local iron trade. The building did not get a castellated appearance until the 19th century when it was given a sandstone shell along with towers and turrets. Shortly after her death in the 18th century Ann Streatfield's ghost was reported to leave Chiddingstone Castle on horseback and canter down to the Inn. By one of the gates she dismounts to negotiate a narrow alley before remounting to traverse the High Street. Despite riding side-saddle she manages to maintain a furious speed. Her appearance is always the same, dressed in a long riding habit and sporting a tricorn hat. A remarkable and unusual thing about this phantom lady is that she much prefers to appear in daylight.

Other local ghosts in the vicinity include:

The aforementioned Anne Boleyn at Hever Castle, where the sad Queen's shade is seen to glide across a bridge over the River Eden in the Castle's grounds. Apparently, but for no apparent reason, she is only seen on Christmas Eve.

Still at Hever there is reputed to be the ghost of a farmer who was murdered for his gold. But as dates and facts concerning the slaying are nearly non-existent I have no great faith that any such happening ever took place.

Leigh (sometimes pronounced Lye) is a couple of miles north-east of Chiddingstone. Here, at a house named Ramhurst, a pair of ghosts plagued an army officer's family in the 1850s. These two made quite regular appearances and seemed to be a married couple. Somehow, and I don't know how, the lady of the house managed a conversation with the couple who were dressed in the adornments of the mid-18th century. The helpful pair explained that their name was Children and they had once owned the house and were very sad to leave it. Research turns up a family named Children who had petered out in 1753. Make of it what you will.

Penshurst, a village worth visiting, is some two miles south of Chiddingstone. Penshurst Place has reports of a spectral lady in ruff and farthingale.

Sir Philip Sydney, who was born here, is reputed to haunt the same house. And a young couple whose love for each other was passionate but socially unsuitable haunt a nearby lane. The outcome of their forbidden romance is unknown.

The Cardinal's Error
Lodge Oak Lane, Tonbridge

The Cardinal's Error at Tonbridge is not easy to find. It obviously pre-existed all the surrounding buildings and now seems marooned on a vast estate. The name refers to Cardinal Wolsey who failed Henry VIII in his greatest diplomatic responsibility, the annulment of the King's marriage to Catherine of Aragon. His dismissal from the chancellorship followed and he died in disgrace, but conveniently before he could be tried for treason.

The Cardinal's Error has only been a pub since 1946; prior to that it was a farmhouse. There is a tale here that beggars belief: nearby once stood a priory and it is suggested that Wolsey escaped to the priory and then on to the then farmhouse, now public house, disguised as a nun. How such a story could exist without the slightest foundation really stretches the imagination.

The relatively well-known ghost of the Cardinal's Error is a lady with a large hat. She is said to look middle-aged and benign and also makes a habit of sitting on beds. Would you believe that there are accounts, verging on the ridiculous, which would have this poor lady acting as a decoy to aid Wolsey's escape? Why can nothing be simple? On several occasions during quite recent history fashion has dictated that the fairer sex wear enormous hats. Who knows, she was probably a kindly aunt who had just returned from Ascot.

I visited the Cardinal's Error on a very fine December day in 2003. It is another 'tardis' pub, far bigger inside than the exterior suggests. I questioned a charming lady behind the bar about the large hatted lady. She had heard the story but had reservations about its authenticity.

"We are in *The Haunted Pub Guide*," she volunteered.

(This is an excellent book by Guy Lyon Playfair.)

"But have you witnessed anything unusual yourself," I enquired.

"All the usual things with a building this age, screaming doors, moaning floorboards, noises that sound like footsteps but could have a thousand simple causes."

"Nothing else?"

"Well, it is funny how you see something in the corner of your eye and you turn quickly but it is gone. I only get it here. Do you know what I mean?"

"I certainly do, young lady. I certainly do."

Whilst in town the avid ghost hunter may be interested in a trio of obscure ghosts mentioned in yet another excellent book, *Ghosts of Kent* by Peter Underwood. Mr Underwood mentions a Tudor house where a spectral collie sits sedately beside a tree on the front lawn, a white shape that scared off hop-pickers in 1920, thought to be a schoolboy joke, and a gatehouse where a mysterious phantom girl appeared in the 1970s.

Tonbridge is a fine place to stay for the established and serious ghost hunter. A triangle fanning out north of the town and yet no further than the M25 will bring the searcher of the supernatural to Westerham. Here, Andrew Green *(Our Haunted Kingdom)* tells of some mild poltergeist activity at Rooks Cottage. The strange but minor occurrences in the 1970s would seem to involve an old man found dead at the bottom of the stairs. Also Quebec House has a tenuous story of Sir James Wolfe's shade and an even more indistinct story of the ghost of Churchill in his favourite armchair at Chartwell.

Slightly further east, the village of Sundridge boasts the ghost of Lady Frederick Campbell. She was burnt to ashes at Combe Bank in 1807. The only part of her body recovered was a small piece of her thumb and periodically Lady Campbell returns in search of it.

Crossing the A21 takes you to Sevenoaks, where Sixties pop idol Vince Hill and his wife were driven from their 17th century coach house by an unknown 'something' that thudded up the stairs.

A few miles north-east the visitor comes across the village of Ightham that straddles the old A25. At Ightham Mote in 1872 a woman's skeleton was found bricked up in a cupboard. These are thought to be the remains of Dame Dorothy Selby. Somehow Dame Dorothy found out about the gunpowder plot and sent an anonymous letter to her cousin, Lord Monteagle, imploring him not to attend Parliament on 5th November 1605. It is thought that Dame

Dorothy was seized by the plotters who exacted a terrible retribution. She was bricked up and left to starve to death. Her spectre is still witnessed and is always preceded by a drop in temperature.

Turning directly south one reaches the tiny and attractive hamlet of Plaxtol. Here the ghost of an 18th century dairymaid haunts the extremely ancient Old Soar Manor. Legend dictates that the unfortunate lass was deflowered by a local family priest. Some type of altercation took place in the chapel of the Manor. The young girl fell unconscious and drowned in a few inches of water. Did she fall or was she pushed? We shall never know but her shade has haunted the chapel ever since.

Nestled between Plaxtol and Shipbourne stands a large house called Fairlawne. In the early 1300s this massive estate belonged to the mighty Culpeper dynasty, as of course did nearly everything else in Kent. The building later passed to the Vane family. In 1662 Henry Vane Jnr. was brought up on a charge of treason and executed on Tower Hill. It is he who haunts Wilderness Walk at Fairlawne, with his head tucked underneath his arm, sometimes he is alone and sometimes he's with his wife. It would seem that she has remained faithful beyond the veil.

It is possible to cut through the back roads to West Peckham from Plaxtol. Here there have been some very strange happenings, many of which occur on Friday 13th. On that day Diamond Cottage, home of murdering highwayman Jack Diamond, was struck by lightning - home and occupant were burnt to a cinder. The ruins remained for many years and a terrifying spectre was witnessed at 6:30 am on May 13th 1961 and on several other anniversaries into the 1980s and 90s. Those that remain long enough describe a fearsome-looking spectre with no legs.

The King's Head, Five Oaks Green

This pub looks a little plain from the outside but internally it is neat and attractive. Unfortunately when I visited there was nobody around who knew anything of the supposed ghostly activity.

The King's Head has long suffered mild poltergeist activity. The usual type of thing: the lifting of glasses, knocks on wood, footsteps, doors being locked and unlocked, bells that ring (despite being disconnected) etc, etc. What is particularly strange however is that one knocking on the back door was extremely animated and violent, lasted for several minutes and was heard from both sides of the door.

Actual sightings of spectral phenomena are fewer in occurrence but by no means non-existent. From time to time a man-sized black blob manifests itself in the bar and works its way across the room. There is also 'the lady'; the shade of a middle-aged lady dressed in a black skirt and white blouse adorned by a large cameo brooch. She has been witnessed by at least four of the inn's previous tenants.

Whilst in the neighbourhood a three to four mile trip south-west will bring the hunter to Southborough where Winton Lodge is thought to be haunted. There have been many strange happenings of a supernatural nature here. The ghost in situ is thought to be Queen Caroline, wife of George IV.

Another few miles to the east lies Pembury where there once stood Old Bayhall Manor. Here there is the intriguing story of the ghost of Anne West, the last mistress of the Manor. But as the house has gone and the ghost has not been witnessed for a number of years I'll say little more except that the story belongs more in the realms of folklore, legend and mythology.

The Red Lion, Rusthall, Nr Tunbridge Wells

I wonder why this rustic old pub with its supposed canine ghost has never been mentioned (as far as I know) by any of my colleagues or by any of the contributors to anthologies on Kent. Why did it take a blue-eyed Berkshire boy to seek it out?

The Red Lion is reputed to hold the oldest licence in Kent. If my memory serves me right it was granted in 1450 but the building is a few years older. Andrew, who is co-tenant with Martin, informed me that apart from the usual - 'cold spots', fridge locking itself, toilet doors locking and unlocking he had come downstairs one morning to see the hindquarters of a dog going through the bar door. Taking umbrage at the audacity of the beast he ran to the door, a matter of yards away, but no animal was in sight. Customers have occasionally reported seeing this spectral canine, a large and scruffy animal, curled up on the floor. It is reputed to disappear before one's very eyes.

Andrew told me that at certain times a chill comes over the place and his dogs become very agitated. On hearing they were Yorkies it

was less of a surprise. I used to have a Yorkie who would become agitated, nay hysterical, if somebody coughed three streets away.

Whilst in the Rusthall district there is reputed to be a clopping, headless horseman wearing armour, he is thought to be one of Cromwell's Ironsiders. Near Broomhill Road, and in the road itself, there are reports of a 'man' who appears to be standing in a hollow where a cottage once stood.

In nearby Tunbridge Wells, Mary Jennings, an enormous woman, reputedly haunts the Common. Massively stout and said to wrestle at fairs, Mary was a tippler of extremes. She died in 1736 at the age of 30.

I am indebted to Peter Underwood *(Ghosts of Kent)* for informing me of: - a premises, once a shop, where some people experience a time warp; phantom footsteps in a period house at Calverley Park and a phantom coach and horses in Auckland Road. Also in Woodbury Park Road, where some orphans were burnt to death, the unfortunate children are occasionally heard banging and thumping. Even less frequently they are heard singing in a choir.

The Star and Eagle, Goudhurst

Goudhurst is one of the most attractive and peaceful villages in Kent. Attractive from its Muscovy duck-adorned village pond to its 13th century St Mary's Church. Perfect peace is only really obtainable in the evening when the relentless traffic ceases winding its way up the hill. On reaching the opposite side of the street safely one feels a sense of achievement. The Star and Eagle is at the top of the High Street near the Church. Incidentally St Mary's was hit by two German landmines during World War II, destroying much of the glasswork. This gives the impression of the building looking more like a fortress than an ecclesiastical structure. The Star and Eagle is a late medieval half-timbered building with leaded windows. It is thought to have started life as a monastic building but was used for a completely different reason in the mid-18th century. Smuggling was rife and the Star and Eagle was a stronghold of the notorious Hawkhurst gang.

In 1747 the good folk of Goudhurst locked themselves indoors whilst a spirited battle took place. The Goudhurst militia had discovered a tunnel that led from the Star and Eagle to the Church. The militia lay in wait in the churchyard after being tipped off that smuggled goods stored in the cellar would be loaded onto asses that evening. A fierce and bloody battle took place. The militia, having the element of surprise, were victorious. Many of the gang were killed or captured, later to hang at Tyburn. Some of the badly wounded tried to make their way back up the tunnel to the inn. It is reported that several died there of their wounds. Over the years, I will admit not recently, customers at the inn had reported low moans and sounds of distress coming from the inn's end of the tunnel. The tunnel was bricked up many years ago but I can vouch for its existence, the year of the battle and the Tyburn hangings. The rest of the above story is a compilation of stories related by various locals.

Whilst in Goudhurst, Joan Foreman *(The Haunted South)* tells a particularly gruesome story. The author relates an episode in which she met an unknown, terrifying and malevolent creature whilst staying in a nearby school. I shall not elaborate, it is Joan's story not

mine and I am rather pleased it is.

A few miles west of Goudhurst lies Lamberhurst, another attractive village. Scotney Castle is reputed to be haunted by a customs man who drowned in the moat. It has been reported and distorted in so many books I will say no more.

Lamberhurst also possesses a spectral dated limousine that is parked on a wooded road. It disappears when one is about a hundred yards from it. At nearby Hook Green the ruins of the once beautiful Bayham Abbey is said to be haunted by phantom monks, ghostly voices and quietly throbbing bells.

A few miles east of Goudhurst lies the small Weald town of Cranbrook. In Frythe Walk the Old Pest House was once used for plague victims but no plague-ridden ghost walks here. The spectral lady, quite often witnessed, wearing a long gown and carrying a candle is thought to be Theresa Benenden. Theresa was the daughter of a 16th century owner. The story goes that her father cut off her annuity for reasons unknown. To get her own back Theresa committed suicide. "That'll learn him." Ever since the lovely lady has haunted the building.

Also, Peter Underwood tells us of an unnamed modern house in the town where the ghost of a young boy was regularly seen. The family decided to tell him, loudly and firmly, to go away, after several weeks he took the subtle hint and went.

The King's Head, Staplehurst

Seen from miles away this impressive building stands beside an old Roman road. Parts of the old inn are said to date back to the 1300s but most of the construction is mid-17th century. There are a couple of tombstones in the back yard that a previous landlord found conducive with his story.

I personally arrived on a bright December morning; there were many such days in the winter of 2003. I had been here before, many years ago. I knew of the supposed hauntings then but was not sufficiently interested to enquire about them. As it was early I settled to sit outside on the roof of the well with a coffee.

"Still got your resident ghost?" I asked the friendly bright barman.

"No, never did have as far as I know," he replied.

"But I have seen reports from some top writers in the field of supernatural phenomenon," I replied, before going on to name a couple.

"Well me and the Guvnor have been here a dozen years and have noticed nothing at all."

"Where did the rumours come from then?"

"The landlord back in the Seventies, he thought it would drum up trade. The only one who ever claimed to experience it was him. Load of bulls**t."

Swiftly moving on.

There is a quite well-authenticated ghost in Staplehurst. It is 'Flasker' Beesley, one of the notorious Goudhurst / Hawkhurst gang. This likeable old smuggler owned a farm near Staplehurst and his spectre is occasionally seen escaping up the chimney from the inglenook.

Directly south of Staplehurst the hunter will find the small town of Sissinghurst. This was the home in the 1700s of Sir Richard 'Bloody' Baker. Baker was Chancellor to Queen Mary which gave him power to indulge in every perversion known to man and access to a great deal of money. At the nearby church there was a dark cupboard known as Baker's hole. Here he tortured and imprisoned protestants before burning them at the stake and claiming their lands. One could write chapters on this English Bluebeard but it is sufficient to say that he came to a sticky and just end and that his ghost haunts the little church and the mighty garish Sissinghurst Castle built nearby.

Peter Underwood *(Ghosts of Kent)* tells the above story in more detail. He relates also a tale of a ghostly priest witnessed by Sir Harold Nicolson at the newly-renovated Sissinghurst Castle and goes to great lengths in a complicated story concerning a house named Brandey.

The Royal Oak, Hawkhurst

As one can see from the photographs of the Royal Oak the old building is going through massive refurbishment. I called there on three occasions, some months apart, to see how things were going and if it were possible to obtain a decent picture. It was explained to me that there had been a fire and as the Royal Oak was a listed building the restoration would have to be exact and painstakingly slow.

Hawkhurst's most famous resident was probably Sir John Herschel, the famous astronomer. Less welcome of course was the famous smuggling gang that was named after the village. However there would seem to be no connection between the resident ghost and the aforementioned wild band of brothers. The spook seems to be a mild-mannered little man who unobtrusively walks through the staff quarters before disappearing through a wall. There is / was a pair of eyes that haunted room 22. They were seen or experienced on several occasions. Staff called him George, whether or not the eyes belonged to the rather timid little man that disappeared through walls is not clear. I am of no doubt that it will be difficult to trace George or room 22 after the metamorphosis.

The Chequers, Smarden

Smarden is the epitome of all that is attractive in the Weald and the villages therein. It was once a market town specialising in the cloth trade. In the 15th century, 66 drapers, tailors, fullers and weavers, tired of high prices and higher taxes followed Jack Cade in his "rebellion of small property holders".

Reading a local history production whilst visiting the Chequers in 2004, I was surprised to learn of another variation on the origin of the Chequers signboard. Most Chequers pubs are called after the board game, it has been around for as long as time, several boards were found in the ruins of Pompeii. Another explanation is that the board was used as a sort of abacus for counting taxes or changing money. A third explanation is that, coincidentally, the two earls who were first employed to grant licences, the Earl of Wick and the Earl of Surrey, both had a chequerboard included in their coats of arms. Obviously it paid to keep in with such powerful figures and many Chequers inns appeared. Sometime the symbol was sycophantically included with another symbol e.g. the Bull and Chequers in Berkshire.

According to local historians a chequer is also the small pearl-like fruit of the wild Service tree or Shadbush, which is unpalatable until rotten. It was used to sweeten the beer. One learns something everyday.

I arrived at the Chequers mid-morning on the first dry day for a long time and the well-swollen River Beult was testimony to this fact. The ground around here retains moisture, a fact that makes me wonder about the validity of the claims that there is a subterranean passage from the Chequers to the nearby church and another to Romden Castle, over a mile away. The Chequers was with no doubt used for smuggling; any hostelry over 150 years of age on the Weald would have found smuggling obligatory.

I had not been to the Chequers for many years, during which time several extensions have been added to the original building, all of which have been very tastefully done. A glass conservatory has been added to encompass diners and a unique brickwork trough is now inhabited by a collection of colourful fish. Of the interior little had changed, thank God.

I interrupted a gentleman having his breakfast, I ordered a coffee but said there was no hurry. Never get between a man and his bacon and eggs. I introduced myself and we chatted about the supposed hauntings.

"That's right," he said, "whatever it is, it appears in bedroom 6. It is supposed to be a soldier who was murdered by an escaped French prisoner during the Napoleonic wars. There was any number of them imprisoned in Sissinghurst Castle."

"Or," I replied (showing my depth of research), "A French escapee prisoner murdered by an English soldier."

"That's correct, nobody knows which way round it is."

I reflected that it is a pity that ghosts seldom speak. At least we would be able to interpret their nationality.

Over the years the spectre has been blamed for a host of minor poltergeist activities. A lady's evening dress was removed from a wardrobe and moved to the other end of the room. A pair of jeans appeared in the same room after disappearing from one next door.

Knives, spoons, forks, cups and plates turn up in the strangest of places and some utensils, not even owned by the inn, have appeared in cupboards and drawers. Sightings have been rare but a guest was terrified by the appearance of a small man who appeared, then disappeared, in her bedroom doorway. Two dogs, one deaf, but both of placid character, became so impatient and upset at certain times a vet had to be consulted. This is the total amount of information I could glean, other than the fact that one of the spectre's peculiarities is that he seems to prefer the months of April and May for his activities. After acquiring some sketchy directions to Elvey Farm Hotel I left.

Immediately south of Smarden lies the village of Biddenden. This pretty hamlet's main claim to fame is that it was the home of the Biddenden maids. The Chulkhurst sisters, Elisa and Mary, were Siamese twins, literally joined at the hip. Reputedly they were born in 1100 and survived until 1134 when they died within six hours of each other. The sisters were tolerably affluent and left the 'Chulkhurst dole' to provide bread and cheese for the poor. However, it is not the charitable sisters who haunt the village, but an attractive young lady in a white ball dress. In 1837, or '38, Susannah Lost, a local winsome beauty, held a ball for her 18th birthday. Her intended, said to be her adopted stepbrother, slighted her all evening by dancing with another local beauty. To get her own back she drowned herself in Ibornden pond. Her ghost, dressed in the white ball gown, haunts the grounds of Ibornden Park on the anniversary of her birthday. The only trouble is that everybody has forgotten the date.

Elvey Farm Hotel, Pluckley

I found Elvey Farm Hotel with great difficulty. My directions from the Chequers had been correct but I had miscounted. Turn right and take the second road on the left I had been told. However what Weald people call a road I call a track and what they call a track I call a muddy footpath. I finally took a chance on a swamped turning near Elvey Lane. I came across a nicely extended building, the original part being centuries older. There was no one about other than a barking dog. I could not be sure I was in the right place until I saw a muddy sign, stating Elvey Farm Hotel, thrown down on the grass. Opening the car window as far as I dared, considering the growling dog, I took several snaps and left.

I had no idea that Elvey Farm Hotel was haunted, nor indeed had I heard of its existence until I saw it mentioned in a small book Andrew Green had sent me, called *Haunted Inns and Taverns*. Mr

Green goes into more detail in his *Our Haunted Kingdom.* He reveals in an interview with the owners in the 1970s the following spiritual activities.

There was a regular smell of burning wool, lights switched on and off, bolts withdrew from their sockets, bales of hay were thrown about and a large three gallon bowl was turned over. Also a large white illuminated ball hovered several feet above the ground before disappearing. This is not an unusual phenomenon in haunted houses. Experts differ as to the cause; opinions vary from confined electrical energy to ectoplasm. Sightings of the offending shade are rare. However, one disturbing sighting was experienced by the lady of the house. She was looking in the mirror in her bedroom when she saw the reflection of a young man in his early twenties, lying on her bed. As she turned he disappeared.

There was a suicide here in the 1850s when a depressed, middle-aged man, decided to end it all. At the time of Mr Green's interview the owner declared that in his opinion the suicide had nothing to do with hauntings.

The strange thing about this case is that the poltergeist / ghost has been nicknamed 'Old Bill' and is supposedly an ancient farm labourer. His shade has been summarily convicted of throwing a horse saddle some yards on several occasions. Circumstantial evidence if you ask me.

The Blacksmith's Arms, Pluckley

As the photograph portrays, this little pub was still in its Christmas regalia when I visited in mid-January. Another little eccentric story I heard about the Blacksmith's Arms (admittedly from another local hostelry) was that the local media were suggesting that playing darts is dangerous. So, taking this to the extreme, the Blacksmith's regulars turned up at their next match wearing hard hats.

But I digress.

Peter Underwood *(Ghosts and How to See Them)* suggests that the ghost of a highwayman, who was run to ground and butchered by a mob, haunts the pavement outside the Blacksmith's Arms. However, most ghost hunters disagree and place the venue for this event at 'Fridd Corner', several hundred yards away.

Another account has the highwayman hiding in a hollow tree and jumping out on unsuspecting victims on a regular basis. The story goes that a traveller had been forewarned about the hidden footpad. Creeping around to the other side of the hollow tree, he drew his sword and thrust it a dozen times into the hollow, killing the highwayman immediately. For many years the spirit of the slain highwayman frequented the darkness near the old tree.

If, as most locals believe, the above events took place at 'Fridd Corner', in no way does this prohibit the Blacksmith's Arms from being included in this book. The phantom coach and horses that travels through the village en route from Charing to Smarden has often been witnessed passing the inn's door.

The Black Horse, Pluckley

This remarkable gaunt old building is reputed to be over seven hundred years old and was once a farmhouse surrounded by a moat, the original Black Horse being a very modest abode surrounded by cottages. The building served as a bailiff's house and Treasury to the mighty Dering estates. There is a story, by no means substantiated, that Lord Dering flung himself through one of its unusual round-tupped windows to escape from Cromwell's troops.

Research had informed me that the Black Horse suffered from a ghostly prankster, a mildly mischievous poltergeist. Articles disappeared for days on end and then reappeared in the most obvious of places. The spirit was described as playfully harmless, almost childlike in its behaviour. The wickedest thing that it had thus far initiated was to throw a valuable dish across the room. The various tenants over the years have treated the shade with the type of resigned tolerance that one adopts when dealing with an irritating and recalcitrant child.

I called into the Black Horse on a crisp January morning. I was pleased to see that the flag floors and imposing fireplaces were still to be admired. There was a small booklet on the bar called *Haunted Pluckley.* I purchased one with my coffee (I was driving) and showed a casual interest to the attractive young lady behind the bar. I have found the casual approach is often the most productive. Expecting to hear some tale of a few indistinctive knockings from our pale and pastel, playful poltergeist I enquired, "And is this place one of Pluckley's many ghostly venues?"

In anticipation of a reply I tossed the pamphlet disconcertedly onto the table and concentrated on my coffee.

"It certainly is," she replied. "We have three and they are very scary indeed. We have an old lady, a young girl and a cat. You can feel their approach and by some unknown means you can discern which is which. There is a tingling, almost choking coldness, which makes you feel sick to your stomach. My other half and I have experienced it at the same time. We only have to look at each other to know when it is happening. It is a sensation that is totally indescribable to anyone who has not experienced it. You wouldn't believe it."

"I would my dear, I would. You are preaching to the already converted."

I drank my coffee and left.

Concerning the pusillanimous spirit of the Black Horse, read Petrifying Spirits.

The Dering Arms, Pluckley

Unfortunately I did not hear about the hauntings at the Dering Arms until I was back home in Berkshire some 90 miles away, so it was sometime before I could get back to the neighbourhood. It was reading Dennis Chambers little booklet *Haunted Pluckley* that informed me about strange goings on at the Dering Arms.

This handsome old building was once a hunting lodge belonging to the mighty Dering family. Its strange and mullioned windows were brought about by decree from one of the early Dering's. Having escaped from Cromwell's troops (see the Black Horse) by jumping through one he made it mandatory that all buildings on the estate had similar fenestration.

The Dering Arms has a resident customer, a benign and friendly little old lady. Dressed in an old-fashioned frock and bonnet she sits in the corner, with an almost apologetic demeanour, and watches the world go by. The old lady is quite a regular visitor and is so substantial that she has often been mistaken for a flesh and blood customer. This quaint old woman remains until she is commented on and then shyly vanishes.

Whilst in Pluckley, the avid ghost hunter may come across one of the many spirited residents of the most haunted village in England. Forgive me for inflicting the list below once again upon the public. It has appeared in literally dozens of books on ghosts, but it would be impossible to omit it from this book. The phrase 'ad nauseam' springs to mind, so whilst in Pluckley lookout for:

a gypsy woman, old, huddled and collecting watercress

a ghostly woman in white near the site of a burnt down mansion

a translucent curly haired boy

a screaming man

a monk who haunts a house named Greystones

a spectral miller who haunts an ancient mill

a man who fell to his death down a clay pit (could also be the screaming man)

Lady Dering who haunts the churchyard

a suicidal schoolmaster who hanged himself

a huge white phantom dog

the shade of a soldier, known locally as 'The Colonel'

a woman in red, imaginatively nicknamed the 'Red Lady'

and, of course, numerous cottages that have experienced blobs, whisperings and footsteps.

Thank you for your patience.

The King's Head, Grafty Green

I got thoroughly lost by taking shortcuts down minute lanes whilst travelling from Pluckley to Grafty Green. Sadly the inn was closed when I arrived. The exterior of the old building is attractive indeed and mentions quite blatantly its inhabiting ghost, Dover Bill.

Dover Bill was a smuggler of some repute who frequented the King's Head. However, after being taken by the revenue men he was 'persuaded' to give up the names of his colleagues. Many were hanged but Dover Bill had bought his freedom, such as it was. Ostracised by the smuggling fraternity, treated like a leper by the villagers and banished from the King's Head, Bill took to the road. He died at Grafty Green, virtually starving to death.

Unable to enter the King's Head during his later life, old Bill's shade seems to have had no problem entering after his demise. He has been sighted near his favourite spot and witnesses state that a distinct atmosphere of abomination, animosity and pure hate exude from the bowed and withered form.

The King's Head has a second apparition, a phantom coach and horses. Apparently with a headless driver, this phantom stage hurtles past the inn door at breakneck speed. Choosing dark and stormy nights this Lenham bound stage detours to visit the grave of Sir Leonelle Sharpe. Sharpe was a chaplain to Queen Elizabeth I, but why on earth a speeding 18th or 19th century carriage should show any interest in a 16th century cleric must be left to conjecture.

Next door to Grafty Green lies the hamlet of Boughton Malherbe. Here the old Rectory has frequently been visited by a hunchbacked monk. The story belongs to Frederick Sanders, an enthusiastic ghost hunter, and is reported in great detail by Peter Underwood *(Ghosts of Kent)*.

To the north-west of Grafty Green, near the village of Broomfield, lies Leeds Castle. Half of this romantic, moated stronghold, is as late as the 1820s but Leeds was initiated by the Saxons then extended by the Normans, Plantagenets and Tudors. What you see today is a delightful mishmash. The castle is haunted by one of our spectral canine friends. The regularly-witnessed 'Black Dog of Leeds' appears to warn of approaching family misfortunes.

White Lion, Farnborough

Actually at Locksbottom, this beautiful old pub has recently and tastefully been modified. Circa 1626 this ancient hostelry must have witnessed a plethora of colourful characters over the centuries. Not the least of which was a landlord back in the early 1960s. Whilst doing renovations he discovered the skeleton of a woman under the floorboards. The skull was complete and adorned by a bullet hole through the forehead. The landlord decided to place the skull on the bar and adapt it into a macabre lamp. The grotesque exhibit shone its light on nervous customers, flanked by a suit of armour and facing a crest of arms, newly painted to serve the eccentric landlord's ego.

It would seem that the spirit of the unknown lady was more content with lying in obscurity beneath the floorboards than being exposed to the inquisitive. All sorts of minor mishaps began to happen around the pub: flying glasses, footsteps, misplaced objects. I am told that the poltergeist activity finely simmered down. Unfortunately I am unable to authenticate this. Also I was unable to see if the skull is still in existence due to the alterations. I shall attempt to revisit shortly.

Whilst in the area in the village of Downe, Downe Court is thought to be haunted. Andrew Green interviewed several victims here. It is thought that a troop of cavaliers hung a man here, which could be the cause of a dark repressive feeling that refuses to be exorcised.

Slightly further to the south-west lies Biggin Hill where the scream of a Spitfire is heard. Assumed to be a victory roll the pilot is thought to be celebrating the successful Battle of Britain.

The Chequers, Bickley

This is an old 16th century pub in the centre of suburbia; its honoured guests have included Charles Dickens, Samuel Pepys, and Dick Turpin, albeit in spiritual form. Poor old Dick has worked far, far harder posthumously than he ever did when he was alive. One day I must have a count up, but I believe the highwayman's spirit has been witnessed in over 50 venues, many of them in districts that he never even ventured into. I am really at a loss as to why on earth it should be presumed that any respectable spirit clad in early 18th century attire is Dick Turpin.

The seldom seen spirit at the Chequers is a man dressed in green velvet, wearing a plumed hat and writing with a quill. I'm not even sure that Turpin could write. The man in green is reputed to stare up as if interrupted and then fade away.

The Chequers also boasts two ladies in 18th century dress. They are rarely seen but on various occasions they have been witnessed

individually and very occasionally together. All very benign stuff. What wasn't so benign was the ex-landlord who told Guy Lyon Playfair *(Haunted Pub Guide)* that he had endured 11 years of door slamming and beds shaking and on these nights he and his wife had got very little sleep. It makes one wonder why they stayed so long.

I turned up at the Chequers one cold day in January. There were two attractive females behind the bar, both slim, dark and with high cheekbones, I took them to be sisters, I was of course wrong.

"Are there any ghosts here?" I enquired.

"Meant to be," one of them replied, "We've been on the telly and all."

"Yes, but have you actually seen anything?"

"He's a tidy ghost," came the answer, "Can't bare to see bottles out of line. He puts them straight. Not like where I used to work, we had an active one there who used to throw the beer mugs about."

"Where was that?" I asked.

"Just up the road, the Queen's Head."

I got directions and made my exit.

I was informed that Bickley's large neighbour, Bromley, had a couple of ghosts. One of them was a Roman Catholic Father who returned to his house and the other was a haunted council house. But as the addresses of both were unknown it would be a very ambitious ghost hunter who tried to follow either trail.

The Queen's Head, Chislehurst

Unfortunately the Queen's Head had not opened when I arrived. I could not tarry long but long enough to chatter to a couple of old regulars. The slightly far-fetched story tells of a regular at the bar (historic time unknown) who was inclined to take advantage of the friendly landlord by putting his drinks on tick. When the pub was sold the new landlord would make no such arrangement. The customer entered one day and demanded a drink with menaces. The new landlord refused and barred the man. Uttering all types of threat he left under duress. The hard up customer's body was found floating in a pond the following day just a stone's throw from the inn.

Over the following years all sorts of mishaps occurred at the Queen's Head, each being blamed on the suicidal customer. Hence the expression 'dying for a drink'.

Unable to verify any of the above I must rely on the Chequers barmaid. The flying glasses could possibly be the poor customer's spirit trying to snatch a drink while the landlord is not looking.

A few miles north-east of Chislehurst in this suburban sprawl lies the village of Bexley, now virtually a suburb of Dartford. Bexley boasts two aristocratic ghosts.

Prince Edward, son of Edward III, and better known as the Black Prince, stayed at Hall Place before distinguishing himself at the Battle of Crecy in 1346. The appearance of his shade is taken to be an ill omen by the residents.

Another spiritual visitor to Hall Place is Lady Constance, wife of the 13th century owner Sir Thomas Hall. When he was accidentally killed Lady Constance, distraught with grief, threw herself off the tower. Her ghost returns to look for her beloved husband.

PS A ghost of lesser social status is the spirit of a young serving girl who frequents an attic bedroom.

The Pied Bull, Farningham

This is the site of one of the many phantom coach and horses that appear in Kent. Apparently the old inn was extended and one of its walls now encompasses part of the old highway. This of course was once the main route from London to Maidstone. Customers have been known to leap from their seats as the sound of a phantom coach careers alongside their tables. Not good for the digestion!

On my latest visit I saw a notice on the wall stating that in 1730 six coaches stopped at the inn each day. Strangely I would have thought this an understatement.

We are also informed that in 1630 landlord Matthias Rage (I knew his brother Tempestuous) secured a 500-year water right for the inn. I chatted to the friendly landlord about the spectral coach. He had seen or heard nothing but admitted to having only occupied the building for five months. We decided between us that the 'phantom flyer' may have opted for the less stressful bypass.

Just a few miles south of Farningham lies Shoreham. Andrew Green *(Our Haunted Kingdom)* tells us of an ancient house at Timberden Bottom. This abode houses not only a phantom lady in black but also an old clown. Rumour states that the clown committed suicide here but from whence the lady in black originated nothing is known.

Further south near to Sevenoaks is the village of Kemsing. Kemsing, on the old Pilgrims road, is haunted by the ghost of the 'repentant knight'. Once a year on a late December evening, a phantom knight rides down to the village church where he dismounts and steps inside. His demeanour is said to be remorseful and reports of weeping have been made. In church this sorrowful man kneels in prayer. The identity of the 'repentant knight' is speculated to be one of the four knights who slew Thomas Becket. Or is it a coincidence that the famous archbishop died at 5pm on December 29th 1170.

Cricketers and King's Arms, Meopham

Dick Bennet could not resist a pretty face. His wife was forever jealous but when he returned from the Napoleonic wars with a fancy French lady named Mademoiselle Pinard and expected his wife to put her up she had had enough. Then, leaving his latest mistress with his wife, Dick returned to the wars. The butt of every lewd joke in the village Bennet's wife made his mistress's life a misery. She beat her soundly and all but starved her to death.

Mademoiselle Pinard could take no more, stuck in a foreign land, unloved by Dick and ill-treated by his wife she decided to end it all. Wearing a bright orange dress, the last decent one the harsh wife had let her keep, she walked to the bottom of Steel Lane by the Cricketers and hanged herself.

Her ghost, uniquely dressed in bright tangerine, has been seen regularly at the Cricketers. The shade of Mademoiselle Pinard had company in the 19th century when a local miller, named Bob Bennet, hung himself. Both have been seen on the green near the Cricketers and the King's Arms.

The George, Meopham

A headless figure, thought for some unknown reason to be a monk, walks between the George and the village church, a distance of some 200 yards. The figure is meant to follow a subterranean passage between the two sites. Personally I am a great disbeliever in underground passages. I never can see what that practical function is. If smuggling is the reason, why bring the contraband 10 miles by road and then by tunnel for the last 250 yards. The expensive construction would not make the enterprise financially viable. Other than to add that although the headless monk has been witnessed at both the inn and the church he is most often seen where two pillars once stood, there is little more to report.

Dean Manor at Meopham was the scene of a BBC radio broadcast in 1936. One of the most accomplished of ghost hunters, Harry Price, conducted some recording experiments but nothing positive was recorded. However, one of the technicians who slept in the house that night swore he had heard footsteps. A second programme was suggested in 1939 after the ghost of a serving girl was sighted. The maid had hanged herself in a nearby ruined granary. However the owner of Dean Manor declined. Not to be outdone the intrepid reporter spent the night as close as he could to the granary. He reported hearing footsteps, an axe like sound, the click of a door lock and finally an ear-piercing scream.

Just to the west of Meopham is the village of Hartley. Richard Treadwell, the 18th century landlord of Fairby House, is seen in the saddle of his grey mare near Fairby Farm.

At Fawkham, Pennis Lane, is reputedly haunted by a nun. She was a victim of Thomas Cromwell's soldiers who, having sated their lustful sexual appetites, cut off the poor nun's head. For many years her skull, unearthed by a ploughshear, adorned the study at Pennis Farm.

A few miles south at Wrotham, Wrotham House was reported in the famous Lord Halifax's ghost book. As long ago as 1879 a contributor wrote to Lord Halifax stating that many strange things had happened to her relatives and herself during a two night stay. Among other things her locked door flew open and a well-dressed man in grey entered. This happened on consecutive nights. Telling her host she could stay no longer she was told that the ghost only appeared three times and then only to strangers. It later transpired that the gentleman in grey had met his demise by being thrown from a window by his brother.

Ye Olde Leather Bottel, Northfleet

I took directions from the centre of Northfleet.

"Just up the hill," I was told. The hill seemed to go on forever.

There have been a couple of spooks reported here but I can glean very little information. Other reports inform us that one is an elderly woman in a matronly cardigan. Often mistaken for a customer this gentle spook makes towards the bar and then dematerialises. The second ghost is a tall, fair, long-haired man; facts about this young spook are virtually unobtainable.

Whilst in Northfleet the reader may try to search out a 1930 council house in Waterdales. The building experienced some poltergeist activity in the mid-1960s. A couple of spirits were regularly witnessed; one was a fair-haired young girl and the other a headless woman. The tenants were forced to leave.

Just down the road at Northfleet's sister village a gruesome tale unfolds. Southfleet Rectory is haunted despite several exorcisms. Over a hundred years of testimony by various rectors leave little doubt that something supernatural exists.

Legend relates that a Priory once stood on the site. Some monks enticed three nuns there. They were raped but their sin was discovered. It was decided that the women had acted in a provocative and coquettish manner. They were condemned to be bricked up in the walls. It is not surprising that the phantom here is a nun. She is described as four feet six inches tall, dumpy and wearing a torn old habit.

Not an immediate turn on one would have thought.

The Ship, Cobham

Richard Dadd, the fourth of seven children, was born in Chatham in 1817. Robert Dadd, his father, was a chemist and his mother Mary Ann had died before Richard's seventh birthday.

The Dadds were a refined, tolerably prosperous middle-class Victorian family. From his early days at Rochester Cathedral Grammar School Richard had shown a pronounced natural talent for art. At the age of 20 he entered the Royal Academy School of Art. Here he won three silver medals and became a member of the 'Clique' associating with such well-known names as Augustus Egg, William Powell Frith, H N O'Neill and John Phillips.

After exhibitions at the Society of British Artists and the Royal Academy, Dadd was taken under the patronage of wealthy solicitor Sir Thomas Phillips. In 1842 Dadd and Phillips set sail on what was accepted in those days as 'The Grand Tour'. It was at this period that Dadd showed the first signs of mental illness. He would rant and rave and had drawn up plans to murder the Pope.

On his return in May 1843 Dadd's condition had deteriorated. He spent most of his time locked in his room living on beer and eggs and indulging himself in painting portraits of his friends with deep red gashes across their throats. In August his condition was so bad several specialist doctors suggested he be confined. His father Robert would not hear of it. All Richard needed was to unburden his mind. Father and son departed for Kent the following day where they booked in at the Ship at Cobham. The pair took an evening stroll together across Cobham Park. It was the last time Robert Dadd would be seen alive.

The following day a butcher, taking a short cut through Cobham Park to Wrotham Market, found a body in Paddock Hole, later to be renamed Dadd's Hole. The body, later identified as Robert Dadd, was covered in razor cuts and knife wounds. The hunt was on for Richard

Dadd. He had, although bloodstained and dishevelled, been able to obtain passage on a boat to France. Dadd might have lain low there had he not attempted to cut the throat of a fellow coach passenger at Fontainebleau. Arrested by the French police he was lodged at Claremont. After much legal wrangling and diplomacy Dadd was extradited and remanded to stand trial at Maidstone assizes.

In August 1844 Richard Dadd was found unfit to plead and was committed to Bethlehem (Bedlam). Several years later Dadd was committed to Broadmoor where he died in 1885. For many years at Cobham, early on a late August evening, two spectral figures leave the Ship Inn. The evening is misty and the figures stroll towards Cobham Park. They seem to be in conversation but nothing is heard. The figures disappear into the encroaching darkness. Some minutes later footsteps are heard running from Paddock Hole, later Dadd's Hole, and the merest outline of a figure can be seen as it hurries east towards Rochester.

The Cooper's Arms, Rochester

Whilst researching this book I found it necessary to spend six or seven nights at hotels in Kent. Bang goes any profit. I stayed in Rochester for a couple of nights and as it was January I had to take pictures in the dark. I used to use the Cooper's Arms quite a lot whilst staying with friends at Gillingham. I had been misinformed and told it was closed down. Thankfully it hasn't. It is a fine pub, one of many in the town.

The Cooper's Arms began life as an 11th century monastery brewery. As the name implies the beer was also barrelled here. It will come as no surprise that the resident ghost is a monk. The spirit, dressed in a grey habit, appears through the wall of the bar and heads for the cellar. He leaves a cold and clammy atmosphere behind him. I count as pure speculation the story that a holy brother was walled up on the premises for some long-forgotten sin. On arriving in January I was pleased to see that the figure of the supposed spectral monk was still in its place by the cellar steps. The young man behind the bar was extremely busy but I got a chance to get a word in while he poured my pint.

"Have you still got your resident ghost?" I enquired.

"We certainly have," he replied. "I came across it just last week, down in the cellar."

"What was it like?"

"It was a fast thing, a thing the shape of a man. It was a type of transparent light grey blob. It went past me very swiftly, everything went cold. It was scary, damned scary."

I had little chance to continue the conversation but I was pleased to hear the old monk is still about. It seems he has lost a little weight and moves far quicker.

The George Wine Bar, Rochester

Another ghostly monk here. A very solid one. The George wine bar was once the George Inn. The cellar that was once a crypt is now something approaching a Thai restaurant. The monk is said to be a short old man dressed in brown and always smiling. Although small he looks unexpectedly solid and has scared the living daylights out of barmen bottling up. One described being so terrified that he couldn't move for several minutes.

I got talking to a barmaid upstairs. The crypt / cellar / Thai restaurant was overflowing. I decided not to go down and try to discuss the resident ghost or take any photos.
"Do you know anything about the ghostly monk?" I asked.
"The one downstairs," she queried.
"So I hear. Have you seen it?"
"I think I caught sight of him once."
"And," I rejoined.
"And, bloody nothing, I haven't been down there since. I'd rather throw in my job."
End of interview.

There is ample choice for the ghost hunter from amongst the plethora of classic apparitions in Rochester. Probably best known is the raven-haired lady dressed in white who haunts the castle. She is Lady Blanche de Warrene the wife-to-be of Ralph de Capo, a crusader. He was tricked out of the castle pursuing retreating rebels. Their leader, Guilbert de Clare, dressed in similar armour re-entered the castle with intent of deflowering the lovely Blanche. De Capo seeing what was amiss grabbed a bow and arrow and loosed a shaft at De Clare. The shot went astray killing the lovely Blanche. Oh well, better death than dishonour. Ever since the shade of Blanche has walked the castle towers.

Rochester's old burial ground is said to be haunted by Dickens. A spectral black monk walks the Lanes near the cathedral. Minor Canon

Row is the home of a rejected lady in white, who carries a baby and sports a noose around her neck. The Elizabethan restoration house boasts the shade of a young female in white. When she disappears another black monk, or possibly the same black monk, takes her place. Dickens appears again at the Corn Exchange clock, apparently only on Christmas Eve. He turns up to wind up the clock and set the hands to midnight. Finally, no lesser personage than Admiral Sir Cloudesley Shovell in 18th century uniform strolls the corridors of the Guildhall.

Just north of Rochester in the village of Shorne, Andrew Green *(Our Haunted Kingdom),* tells us of several apparitions at Shorne Lodge. An old man with a brown dog has been witnessed, as has a peculiar mist. Another spectre is a young lady who is thought to have died from a throat infection in the 17th century.

At Higham, between Shorne and Rochester, Frederick Sanders reported to Peter Underwood *(Ghosts of Kent)* on a ruined mansion known as Great Hermitage. Great Hermitage is a local name applied to the gloomy remains on Higham marshes. Some of the spooks witnessed here include a phantom horseman riding at great speed. His wrists are chained and it is assumed he is escaping from somebody. There was once a bloodstain that came from a butchered black servant; the stain could not be washed away. A smiling lady, an artist who left a curse and the inevitable indispensable black monk.

Joining Rochester is Chatham. If I remember correctly there is a line between two terraced properties saying where one ends and the other starts.

Chatham is famous for its dockyards. It also has a famous ghost, the limping ghost of St Mary Barracks. Known as Peg-leg Jack he is obviously ex-naval. But seeing as this particular phantom has been mentioned in every ghost book for years I shall say no more.

Andrew Green informs us 122 High Street is haunted. Peter Underwood tells us that an ex-cinema is the haunt of an old commissionaire dressed in a green uniform and Anthony D. Hippisley Coxe *(Haunted Britain)*, informs us that two adjoining houses in Magpie Road may or may not be haunted.

The Upper Bell,
Bluebell Hill, Nr Rochester

I travelled out to the Upper Bell one morning whilst staying at Rochester. The old place looked gaunt and alone. Gone are the days when 10,000 vehicles a day passed along the narrow road that wound its way forever upwards from the A20 to the A2. I pulled great lorry loads of building material over this hill, each time frustrated by holidaymakers with their overheated radiators. Those were the days. The events that follow are reputed to have occurred just outside the Bell's back door.

In the 1880s a travelling butcher, complete with horse, frequented the area. A fine horseman by all accounts. For reasons unknown this butcher saw fit to murder a youth he had been meeting in the woods at the back of the inn. Speculation exists as to what caused the rift and subsequent murder. Suggestions have been made that there was a debt involved. Others implied, tongue in cheek, that there had been a sexual confrontation; you know - a row over a sausage.

For many years Rochester and Chatham groups have been trying to verify the story. Surely if it had happened as recently as the 1880s there would have been sufficient newspaper coverage. Also there's no record of the perpetrator being arrested and taken to court as far as my inquiries go. What there has been over the years are many instances of people witnessing a ghostly horse and rider. Legend insists that this is the 'galloping murderer' returning to the scene of his crime.

The road in front of the Upper Bell has witnessed a strange series of events. As mentioned before, it was narrow, dangerous and extremely busy. Literally dozens of fatal accidents had occurred here before its widening.

Bluebell Hill has experienced a long-running spate of the vanishing hitchhiker syndrome. Apparently numerous drivers have picked up a young lady, only to have her disappear before reaching her destination of Rochester. We have heard it all before, but have we?

In 1974 a motorist hit a young girl who had walked blatantly out in front of him. This being long before the time of personal mobile phones, the driver decided to wrap her in a blanket and carry on to Rochester police station. He returned with several officers. They retrieved his blanket but there was no sign of the girl. When the above story was printed in the local press upwards of a dozen motorists wrote in with similar tales of the phantom hitchhiker of Bluebell Hill. Some had given the young lady a lift; others had struck the phantom and had apparently carried on without reporting the incident.

In November 1965 a party of four young girls were driving to a pub (probably the Upper Bell) where they had arranged to meet the fiancée of one of their number. On a sharp bend on Bluebell Hill the car skidded and turned over, three of the girls were killed and the fourth was seriously injured. Taking a consensus of descriptions from the many drivers who have witnessed the spectre investigators were able to establish the probable name of the girl who hitchhikes along the A229 over Bluebell Hill.

Nearby Maidstone seems totally devoid of haunted inns. However, Peter Underwood *(Ghosts of Kent)* apportions considerable space to a feeling of depression experienced by one of his correspondents in Maidstone museum. The venue is the Baxter print room. Facts are virtually non-existent other than the writer's description of a feeling of deep dejection and melancholy apparently motivated by the situation of several prints. Personally I found the report just a little superfluous but the theory stated at the end was adroit, intriguing and worthy of much discussion.

The Black Boy, Upper Halling

From Bluebell Hill I returned to the M20, proceeded west to the next junction and left on the A228. It runs parallel to the A229 and in the old days had similar hazards. I passed through Snodland, where there was the horrendous murder of a police officer in 1873. The inquest was heard at the Bull. Unfortunately there has not been the faintest whisper of anything supernatural.

Onto Halling and finally Upper Halling which is reached with a sense of achievement. I was dismayed to find the Black Boy had been closed for some time. The building looked respectable but empty, the badly peeling sign squeaked in the breeze. Being unable to obtain any face-to-face research I must rely on Andrew Green's *Haunted Inns and Taverns.* The landlord in 1991 wrote to Mr Green stating that he had some poltergeist activity. A glass washing machine was turned on overnight and there was a definite presence in the bathroom. The ex-landlord goes on to relate how he was down in the cellar one day when he heard footsteps behind him. He turned to see a mature lady in red. Thinking it to be his mother he inquired as to her wants. There was no reply. A few seconds later he returned to the lounge above. There he found his mother still comfortably ensconced in an easy chair. One assumes she was not dressed in red. Strange!

The Black Bull, Cliffe

I had not been to Cliffe for many years and knew little about the Black Bull. I knew it was supposed to be haunted but it was very minor stuff, doors opening, unknown footsteps etc, etc. I located three other pubs in this prettiest of villages but the Black Bull I could not find. A large building on a corner had all the appearances of once having been licensed premises so I enquired of a passing lady who was walking her dog.

"Yes, that was the old Black Bull," she replied, "It is being altered into two private properties."

What a forlorn and frighteningly true statement that is, it is happening everywhere. I left my colleague to take a couple of photographs and went back to the car to write up some notes. This was the second closed pub I had found that day. What was I going to write on it? I knew it was built on a graveyard and quite probably the graveyard was built on a Roman site. Fertile ground this for producing spooks.

At this point a lady walked up the road and asked my colleague why she was taking pictures. She explained the situation and asked the newcomer if she was the caretaker.

"No," she replied, "I am the owner. Would you like a look around?"

I jumped at the chance and was given the five dollar tour. The interior had been immaculately transformed.

"Would you like to see the well?" She inquired.

I had no idea that it had one but it certainly had. A very clear and deep one, which descended from the transformed cellar. A surround had been tastefully constructed and the well was obviously earmarked as a conversation piece.

"Did anyone drown in it?" I asked

"Not as far as I know. Why do you ask?"

"Well apparently there is some sort of psychic anomaly here. Have you personally experienced anything?"

"Not as yet, but I haven't moved in yet. I will let you know."

She handed me her card - Sylvia Kus, I read. I thanked the lady and started to leave.

"You know about the suicide, I suppose."

I admitted I did not.

"Yes, a chap hung himself, just above the cellar. He was the uncle of one of the old customers here."

I thanked Ms Kus for the added information and drove away.

A couple of miles to the east lies the village of Cooling which is reported to have a haunted churchyard. The village was used as Pip's home in Dickens *Great Expectations.*

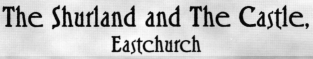

The Shurland and The Castle,
Eastchurch

The Isle of Sheppey is a creature of contradictory moods. On a fine day it is pleasantly empty and mind absorbing and on an overcast one it is desolate, friendless and unfriendly. I was pleased it was in its former mood when I arrived in January. Eastchurch has a phantom coach and horses that glides past the church and down the High Street. Ergo between the Shurland and the Castle. Tenuous I will admit and justifiably so because the most recent report was from a man leaving the Shurland and heading for the Castle. I made some half-jocular enquiries in both pubs, everyone had heard the tale but nobody had had any personal contact.

As I enjoyed a pint in the Castle I spotted a notice on the wall documenting another legend. A legend endorsed by R H Barham in his *Ingoldsby Legends*.

In 1300 Sir Roger de Shurland, Lord of Sheppey, put his sword through a monk who had defied him. The blow was immediately fatal. The local sheriff had the knight surrounded but he escaped by swimming out with his horse into the Thames Estuary. There he

boarded a ship belonging to Edward I. He begged and received a pardon. Returning with his horse to the Sheppey shore he was met by a deformed hag. The bent old crone pointed at the knight and prophesied that his horse had saved his life and would also cause his death. To show his contempt the tempestuous Shurland drew his sword and decapitated his horse. A little ungrateful one would have thought.

Some years later Sir Roger was walking along the beach when he half tripped over a long equine skull. Enraged he gave the skull an almighty kick, injuring his toe in the process. The injury became poisoned and the knight died an agonising death soon after. Sir Roger has an effigy above his grave at the Abbey Church at Minster. It shows the tempestuous knight and close to his right foot is the head of a horse.

PS Never kick a gift horse in the mouth.

The Isle of Sheppey hit the headlines in 1981. In Sheerness a Victorian house owned by a young couple experienced some very animated poltergeist activity. Eventually the phenomena became too disturbing so an exorcism was performed. The spectre wouldn't budge, so the young couple did. The mystery is still unsolved.

One theory emerged from the locals. The house belonged to Harry Morgan, who lived and died alone, his body not being discovered for several days.

Could Harry be getting his own back on an uncaring world?

The George, Newington

Guy Lyon Playfair did an in-depth interview here. He was told by the young couple who ran the establishment that their very young daughter had a friend, 'a man with a hood and skirt'. The young landlady did not dismiss this is as childish fantasy as she had glimpsed the Grey Monk herself as had several customers, one refusing stay in the George any longer.

There were several examples of minor poltergeist activity such as pictures coming off hooks and cutlery being knocked off the table. Dogs refused to go down the cellar whence the phantom emanated.

The family decided to call their benign phantom monk Brother David. An imaginative legend began to emerge, possibly much embellished by the regulars. Brother David was the nephew of the previous Earl of Rochester. He was caught in a compromising position with a nun. Brother David was stripped and thrown into a well in the back garden and his now pregnant nun friend was bricked up alive. To his credit Mr Playfair states that the legend does not seem to be the very well documented, if at all. So there we have it - a greatly exaggerated story.

When I found the George at Newington it was boarded up and had obviously been in a fire. As the traffic was heavy I pulled in further down the road where an ancient rustic was clipping his hedge. I was not sure I had the correct building and wished to confirm this. The

rustic left his tools and came over as I opened the window. He knelt beside the car as if he was going to make an afternoon of it.

"Is there a pub called the George around here?" I enquired.

There was a long silence.

"You've just drove past it. Top of the hill."

"The burnt out place?"

Another long silence.

"Yep, been like it for years, a dodgy insurance job if you ask me."

"Did you ever use it?"

"Every night. Now I goes over to the Bull."

"Did you ever see the ghost?"

A long pause.

"Nope, but I heard it."

"What the monk? You heard Brother David."

"Noooo. That were a lot of old twaddle. I heard the bird."

"Bird! What bird?"

The rustic was getting frustrated.

"The parrot! The bleeding parrot."

"There was a ghostly parrot?"

"Sure were. The bugger died in the May and you could still hear him squawking as Christmas."

I thanked the gentleman and continued on my way.

The avid ghost hunter might like to slip down the road to Bowater's Kemsley Mill, which is reputed to be haunted. In Sittingbourne itself a Georgian bow-fronted property sports the ghost of an unidentified lady. A brewery that once stood in the High Street and later reincarnated itself firstly as a theatre and then a bingo hall is haunted by a brewery worker who fell into a vat and drowned. What a way to go!!

The Windmill, Hollingbourne

This is one of the pubs close to the Pilgrims Way from which the spectral horseman has been seen. Unfortunately not since the 1960s has the ghostly rider been sighted but the clatter of cantering hooves has been heard on a number of occasions. John Harris *(Ghost Hunters Road Book)* names the phantom horseman as a man called Duppa. Duppa lived at Hollingbourne House and was famous for his accomplishments as a rider. On taking a bet he could leap his own wrought iron gates he died in the attempt.

It was along a nearby stretch of the A21 that Maud Ffoulkes, co-author of *True Ghost Stories* gave a lift to an eccentric fellow author Alfred Louis, who was hitchhiking from London to Hythe. There was a rudimentary conversation between Maud Ffoulkes, her chauffeur and Louis on a trip that lasted about 12 miles. Near a small wood Louis requested that they pull over for him to get out. With a weary wave he bade them goodbye. On returning home the authoress learnt that Louis had died several days previously.

The Ringlestone Tavern,
Harrietsham

I had been informed that the Ringlestone Tavern was at Harrietsham. There is a signpost to it on the A20 at Harrietsham that's for sure, but it states a distance of 2.5 miles. After travelling approximately half a mile along the route one finds a second sign stating three miles. This is a little disconcerting but after striving for that distance, uphill for most of the way, along very narrow roads the Ringlestone Tavern comes into sight. As far as I can fathom we are now in a hamlet with the charming name of Wormshill.

The trip is worth it. The end justifies the means. This is one beautiful old inn. Built as many others were, as a hospice for monks in the 16th century, its beams and open fires welcome one in. Apparently the welcome was not always so assured. Not so very long ago an attractive mother and daughter ran the inn. They were very choosy about their clientele. Potential customers would be met and vetted at the door by mother and daughter, who were attired in full evening dress and gloves. The daughter carried a shotgun to dispatch unwanted guests. Unfortunately I can glean little more than I already knew about the ghost. He is never seen but often heard. He stomps, not treads, up the stairs then removes one boot and shies it in the corner of the room. Apparently the second boot never follows. The hard treading shade is reputed to be either a smuggler, a robber, a carefree lover, a murderer or an ex-landlord. Personally I go for the former landlord.

Here is a little scenario based on absolutely no evidence whatsoever.

The landlady, fed up with the landlord's nocturnal drinking bouts with his mates, retires to bed. As she leaves she warns him about making a noise as he comes to bed. Hours later the landlord full of booze, arrogance and confidence ascends the stairs stomping on each one in defiance.

'Who's bloody pub is it anyway. I'll make as much noise as I like.'

Unsteadily gaining the bedroom he flops on the bed beside his adoring wife. Kicks off one boot and then falls asleep.

Well, we've all done it!

Should one eventually find one's way back to the A20 at Harrietsham turn west to Maidstone and in a few miles ask for Eyhorne Manor. The old Manor was / is open to the public. Among its many inexplicable ghostly occurrences is a piece of wood, unseen, but heard slithering across the floor. There is also the inevitable grey lady and a man in black who watches people doing gardening. An indoor poltergeist plays with knives, scissors and tin openers sometimes leaving them in mid-air. Finally there is a playful exterior sprite who snatches clothes pegs from the line.

The Swan, Charing

This is once again a tale of a phantom rider. The Pilgrims Way is littered with them. A very friendly one is this, complete with cowboy hat. The spectre has been known to ride along beside walkers, riders and cyclists. He has a beard and a winning smile. One almost definite sighting was outside the Swan in the Seventies. The spirit doffed his hat and spoke soundless words to a cyclist.

The Swan is a 1930s Tudor building standing where the A252 forks off to Canterbury from the A20. I did not enter, I had been there before and all the spectral interest lies outside.

What I did notice was an advertisement for Montana Mick's Rib Room. Perhaps an enterprising landlord has taken advantage of passing labour.

The Shipwright's Arms,
Hollowshore, Nr. Oare, Faversham

If the Shipwright's Arms isn't haunted then somebody at the ghost agency isn't doing his or her job. The setting is perfect. The melancholy and desolate marshes between the creeks of Faversham and Oare and the occasional foghorn from the Swale are a perfectly staged setting for powerful and mysterious hauntings.

As one might expect the spectre here is a Victorian seafaring man, bearded and wearing high sea boots and a reefer jacket. The spectral seaman was reported to have been shipwrecked in the creek and fought the mud flats and marshes for hours, heading for the only light for miles, the Shipwright's Arms. Dying from fatigue and exposure, just a few yards from the inn, his spectre reportedly haunts the old place. The ghostly mariner has been witnessed in the bar and also standing at the end of the landlady's bed. The ancient mariner appeared on three consecutive nights in the '60s. Also, he is one of a few ghosts that give off an aroma! A strong and not too pleasant mixture of rum, tobacco and ammonia, so I am told.

The weather was too bad for me to visit the Shipwright's Arms in 2004. But I am not cheating. I was there in 1970 when the above hauntings were well substantiated by the landlord and half a dozen locals. However, when I returned in 1999 the owner had experienced nothing paranormal whatsoever.

Peter Underwood *(Ghosts of Kent)* tells us of a nearby house which is haunted by a schoolgirl in Elizabethan dress.

Fox and Hounds,
Herne Common, Herne

One of the most depressing feelings of writing a book like this is discovering the number of inns that are no longer standing or have changed from their intended function. Such a sad case is the Fox and Hounds.

Finding the location very hard to determine I enquired of villagers in Herne High Street and customers in various shops. Finally I found an aged lady who remembered. She informed me that the building was still there but it had been transformed into two semi-detached cottages.

I finally found the building, far out of Herne. It had a stack of fairground equipment behind it and was obviously owned by showmen. The late Jack Hallam first brought the rather scary hauntings to the attention of the public. For many years a family named Bennett owned the inn. The son of the landlord in the mid-1930s was a 12 year-old boy named Philip. Philip was away most of the year at a Catholic boarding school. However, he did spend most his holidays at the Fox and Hounds. On one of these occasions he

awoke to find a grotesquely deformed woman at the foot of his bed. The face and hands had been extremely badly burnt.

Terrified of such a visitation recurring young Philip spent as many school breaks away from home as possible. This did not stop a further five visitations to the petrified boy over the next few years. His mother, who had glimpsed the figure herself, was in some sympathy with the lad, but his father would have none of it and put it down to youthful imagination. Philip noticed that the terrifying spectre was preceded by a wall of coldness on the landing and the aroma of burnt flowers or feathers. When the teenager was forced to sleep at the inn during the absence of his father he thought it prudent to take a shotgun to bed. He awoke to find the terrifying figure at the foot of his bed. He blasted it with pellets and it disappeared. His father was less than pleased to see the state of his wardrobe.

Finally the family left the inn.

Years later Bennett called at the Fox and Hounds and enquired after the awesome ghost. He was told that the young boy there had witnessed the terrifying spook on several occasions. His sister, a girl of 19, had smelt the burning feathers and experienced the cold wall. Some years later he returned yet again and was told that his previous visit had brought forth a spout of unfriendly poltergeist activity. Apparently the lady did not appreciate being enquired after.

Here we must leave it, but it surprises me that none of the many ghost writers who have reported this case have ever tried to find the history of the building. Was a lady burnt to death there? Was the culprit a young boy? A breed she seems to loathe.

Here's a theory based on the scant evidence.

A small mischievous young boy thinks it amusing to set fire to his mother's feather boa whilst she is wearing it. The lady either dies or is terribly disfigured by the outcome. Her spirit hates all small boys after her death and does its best to scare the living daylights out of them.

It's an idea anyway.

The Ship Inn, Herne Bay

Here's a good old rip-snorting, bloodcurdling tale from North Kent.

Early on Easter Monday morning in 1821, the notorious North Kent gang were unloading smuggled goods from their boat at Herne Bay. They were suddenly disturbed by a group of blockade men, led by the courageous, if foolhardy, Sydenham Snow. Although his men were outnumbered 20 to 1 Snow proceeded down the beach. The North Kent gang fired on the gallant lieutenant hitting him in the thigh and shoulder. Snow attempted to fire back but his pistol jammed. Undeterred he drew a knife and headed for the gang, but fell after receiving more wounds. He lay on the beach whilst the gang held his three comrades at bay. Having completed the unloading the blockade men were permitted to carry their leader to the nearby Ship Inn. Despite the attempts of a naval doctor to stem the bleeding Snow passed away the following day. Before his death he and his three companions provided descriptions of the gang. Five were

arrested. Unfortunately prosecution witnesses broke down under cross-examination, (they had probably been threatened) and the five men walked free.

Snow's grave can still be seen in Herne churchyard and early on an Easter Monday they say that three murky figures can still be seen carrying a fourth between them. If you should be unlucky enough to be within earshot you'll hear the low groans of a man in agony. The small party crosses the road and then disappears into the courtyard of the old Ship Inn.

Not long ago I walked from the Ship Inn to the Reculver Towers. Believe me it is a damned sight further than it looks. The Reculver Towers are impressive, even if the atmosphere is badly blighted by a massive caravan site. The ghostly cries of children were long reported from the old Roman fort adjoining the towers. Comparatively recent excavations unearthed the skeletons of no less than 11 young children.

The Court Mount Hotel,
Birchington

I am totally indebted to Andrew Green *(Our Haunted Kingdom)* for this little story. The ghost is/was a pleasant and benign one, she is/was also a beautiful one.

The spectral lady is known as the 'early caller' because it is at 3am when she suddenly appears in a room that overlooks the main road. The haunting beauty is said to have long blonde hair and is attired in a flowing white dress. Mr Green informs us that in the late '60s two gas board executives were staying in the haunted bedroom, obviously unaware of its reputation. As per habit, at 3am the beautiful lady appeared. Apparently, neither one was shocked as the lady seemed to radiate an air of peaceful tranquillity. If anything the pair were a trifle disappointed when the vision disappeared. Little has been seen of late but footsteps have been heard and Andrew Green mentions rumours of a suicide in the 18th century, but points out that they are unsubstantiated. Personally I believe the spectre to be too serene to have been the shade of a depressive suicide.

I had had a bad day for pubs when I arrived at the Court Mount Hotel in February 2004. I had been unable to reach the Shipwright's Arms, the Fox and Hounds was no longer an inn, although the Ship at Herne was still thriving. On reaching Birchington I found that the Court Mount Hotel was still there, in fact it had been extended, but it had also been turned into offices selling mobile homes.

The Northern Belle, Margate

I had heard that the Northern Belle had closed down before I arrived, albeit from an estate agent friend of mine in Margate. When I did arrive I found it was not only open but thriving. It just goes to prove that estate agents always tell the truth! Perhaps she didn't want me calling on her.

The Northern Belle is in Mansion Street; it is the oldest pub in the town. It is close to the harbour and its old cellars are thought to connect to subterranean tunnels that were used by smugglers. It is in the cellars and also in the bar that the ghost has been witnessed. The apparition is described as a deadly white young female dressed in a shroud. I asked the busy Cockney-sounding landlord about the pale and rather insipid looking spectre.

"I have heard the stories," he replied, "but I have been here several years and seen nothing."

And then I inquired about the cellars.

"Yes they are still there," he replied. "They are extensive and blocked off. I've no idea where they lead."

Realizing I would glean no further information I enjoyed my pint in good local company and then set off to spend the night in Canterbury.

Whilst in town the old Theatre Royal has long been associated with several hauntings. Now disused and probably ready for demolition the resident shade of Sarah Thorne, the famous Victorian actress and one-time owner of the building, will probably soon have to move on.

Just south-east of Margate in the beautiful old Dickensian town of Broadstairs, Thanet House is reputed to be haunted. Here the homebound spirit is thought to be that of a gardener who died at his work.

A little further south, near Acol in Minster, a lady who was incarcerated by her cruel husband haunts Cleve Court. There are also rumours of people experiencing time slips here.

Further south, still at Cliffs End, one comes across a crossroads where a gibbet once stood. One or several of the unfortunates who shuffled off their mortal coil here have been witnessed. There are also unexplained road accidents.

Finally, yet again south, a troop of phantom Roman soldiers is supposed to haunt Richborough Castle.

Canterbury

It struck me that I had never read in any ghost books, books on Kent, or even books on Canterbury of any haunted pubs in the town. Given the age and esteemed veneration of most the hostelries I was most surprised. Over all these years and different volumes had nobody researched this?

I booked into the Falstaff for two nights (thereby ensuring that I would make no profit on this book) and set off through the walled inner town.

I walked from the Westgate, along St Peter's Street, the High Street, St Margaret's Street, St George's Street, Lower Bridge Street, Burgate Lane, Butchery Lane, Mercery Lane, Palace Street, the Friars, back into St Peter's Street and home to the Falstaff. There were dozens of bar cafés but very few pubs. What has happened to this ancient town, this cathedral city?

Had I wanted a drink at Ask, the Orange Kafe, Zizzy's, the Bar Eleven, etc, etc I would have been spoilt for choice, but I was looking for ancient inns.

The few inns I did find were not forthcoming with the slightest hint of supernatural visitations. I tried the Westgate; it is a building as old as time and one of two good Wetherspoon houses in town. But there was nothing. There had been no reports at the Carpenters Arms, which having been told was haunted had detoured to especially. At the ancient Thomas à Becket the chatty landlord shook his head but bought me a drink. The Hobgoblin was a blaze of noise so I couldn't get round to asking. At an ancient inn opposite the Theatre I faired no better. In Casey's Irish bar, which I had entered dubiously, I was pleasantly surprised to be told they had spirits a plenty, but all in bottles. I settled for a very large Jameson's and gave up the ghost.

The Falstaff, Canterbury

The Falstaff stands across the road from Westgate, which is said to be the finest gateway in the country. It is just outside the walls and was originally built in 1403. Pilgrims arriving after curfew were locked outside the gates with nowhere to sleep but the fields and ditches. Some Middle Ages entrepreneur realised the opportunity here and the Falstaff came into being. In the courtyard one is greeted by a group of grotesque heads peering from a wall. The origin is too lengthy to go into here and I am sure it's been reported a couple of hundred times in other books. Suffice it to say that the heads are a little disconcerting when one is having a beer in the courtyard on a warm day.

"This is a very old inn," I said to the chamber lady as she was stacking pillowcases in the upstairs passage.

"Certainly is, Sir, 1403."

"And have you a house ghost?"

"Certainly have, Sir."

"And what shape does it take?"

"They say it is a monk, Sir. But he's gone in a flash, you only see him for a split second."

"Have you ever caught a glance of him?"

"No, Sir, and I don't want to. Ben at the bar knows far more about it." End of conversation.

Ben introduced himself as I had one of several pre-dinner drinks.

"I hear you know all about the ghost, Ben."

"Not really, it's meant to be a monk, but he disappears in a flash."

"Have you ever seen him, Ben?"

"I thought I did once but I wasn't sure."

Nobody seemed to know the identity of the monk if indeed monk it is. One of the most infuriating things that can happen to a researcher is that he is informed of a haunting in an area that he believed he had already covered thoroughly. The young man went on to tell me a convincing story about a pub in Paddock Wood called the

Bluebell or Blue Bell, I shall return there if I have time.

Outside the Falstaff two days later.

Not being sure of the quickest way to the A28, Ashford Road, I asked an elderly gentleman for directions. He answered me in a voice honed by Wellington College and Sandhurst. After directions we got into a short conversation. He knew the Falstaff well. I asked him if he had seen the ghost.

"The monk," he replied, "Several times, in quick succession years ago. I haven't seen him lately though."

"He doesn't hang about, does he."

"No, he seems to appear and disappear in a split second."

I thanked him for his information and bade him good day.

The County Hotel, Canterbury

This is a large and prominent hotel in the centre of Canterbury. It belongs to a well-known group and I came across it on a lunchtime pub crawl. The non-residents bar is large, sedate, interesting and friendly. After chatting to the barman for several minutes I enquired if the old place was haunted.

"I believe so," replied the barman.

"Oh, by what or whom?"

In the next few minutes I was to learn that the offending spirit was a mischievous nun whose worst offence was to move guests' watches from bedside tables. But apparently things got a little more traumatic. Several guests died at the hotel, ostensibly of natural causes and on different dates in different years. Bearing in mind the amount of elderly visitors that Canterbury entices, several deaths at a large central hotel would not seem unlikely.

The barman went on to inform me that a guest experienced something very scary in bedroom 11. Reportedly his hair stood on end and he refused point blank to enter the room again. The guest was escorted to another bedroom, his clothes being fetched by staff.

The Cherry Tree, Canterbury

The Cherry Tree in White Horse Lane has a sincere claim of being Canterbury's oldest inn. Part of the building dates back to 1372, with the remainder being constructed in the mid-1800s. The inn's original name was the Fleur de Lis Tap, being the poor man's bar for the hotel of that name that once existed on the High Street. Incidentally, the County Hotel now stands on the site.

I came across the Cherry Tree virtually by accident after leaving the County Hotel. I chatted briefly to the barmaid, Lydia, and enquired about any hauntings.

"We have got several," she replied. "The most regular one is Gilbert."

"Is somebody inquiring about the ghost?" asked the landlord, Nigel.

He then went into some detail.

Gilbert was the nickname for a wizened little spirit that seems to make irregular appearances. Sometime in the misty past Gilbert was murdered on the premises. A newspaper reported at the time, 'a weary traveller was being set upon by five vagabonds and they did stab him to death.' The vagabonds were later hanged.

Gilbert seems to be a spirit with mood swings. When upset he causes light bulbs to blow. Not long ago he had a particularly tempestuous time and blew nine in one week. There is also an invisible phantom cat here. It is assumed to belong to Gilbert but I'm not sure why. Various guests have felt the cat rubbing against the back of their legs. Nigel also informed me that a bedspread was witnessed ruffling up, just as though a cat was scratching on it.

I meandered outside with the landlord. He showed me his inn sign, which is unusual as it has a different painting of the Cherry Tree pictured on either side of the board. He also showed me an ancient cherry tree.

The board is very unusual but by no means unique. We have one called the Bull's Head in Berkshire, that has the animal's head on the board's frontside and the animal's rear on the board's backside, but I deviate.

The above mentioned ghosts, Gilbert and the cat, are included in a pamphlet Nigel puts out about his pub. It also mentions that the original site was owned by Thomas Becket and that Dickens penned some of his memoirs here.

I was just leaving when Nigel mentioned the little boy. In the early seventies the owner was leaving the premises for pastures new. The removal men noticed that their endeavours were being scrutinised by a little boy. He just stood there staring and saying nothing. When they had all but finished they enquired as to where the small boys' room was. Toys and children's furniture had been noticeably absent.

"What small boy?" asked the owner. "There is no small boy here."

When I first wrote this I used the phrase 'little boys' room', but I altered it as it may have invoked the wrong connotations.

There is no shortage of ghosts in unlicensed premises in Canterbury.

Archbishop Simon Sudbury reputedly haunts the Sudbury Tower. He was the victim of mob violence instigated by Wat Tyler and his Kentish men in 1381. Incidentally, Sudbury's body lies in Canterbury but his head is buried in the church of St Gregory's at Sudbury, Suffolk.

Nell Cook haunts the dark entry within the precincts of the Cathedral. Nell, a servant girl, poisoned her master, the Cathedral canon and his niece after she discovered them misbehaving. I think there was a touch of jealousy here. If so, she paid dearly for it. She was tried, executed and buried under the paving in the dark entry. (See *Ingoldsby Legends*).

An unseen hand allegedly restrains people in the Chapter House.

Peter Underwood tells us that somebody wrote to him claiming to have seen a phantom verger in the chapel of Our Lady Undercroft. The writer was attending a lecture there and noticed the figure in a cassock. After some enquiries he was told that he had probably witnessed Becket's shadow.

Mr Underwood tells us of phantom horses' hooves galloping across the cobbled yard of a nearby manor house. Also of a ghostly monk with a crippled arm in Burgate. Later, during some excavations in the precinct, a skeleton with a broken arm was discovered.

The extremely picturesque Weavers House beside the river is reputed to be haunted. It certainly is the correct setting. It was built in 1561 by a rich merchant to accommodate persecuted refugee weavers from Holland.

A few miles outside of Canterbury on the A28 lies the village of Chartham. I have a tenuous association with the village as a very good friend of mine's grandfather owned a sweet shop there. It is said that yet another monk haunts Howfield Manor. The Manor is allegedly built on the site of an old monastery. During a fire at the monastery a brave monk saved several others before expiring himself. The chant of voices is supposedly heard here but what they have to do with the brave brother I cannot ascertain.

Joan Foreman *(The Haunted South)* tells us of a haunted cottage here. Back in 1975 there was pronounced poltergeist activity here. It became so bad that the Bishop of Dover was brought in to perform an exorcism. The outcome is not recorded.

The Red Lion, Wingham

The Red Lion stands in a prominent position on the Canterbury to Sandwich Road. I was too early for it to be open when I last arrived. No matter, I have called in before on several occasions, albeit 25 years ago. I do not doubt that it still has the session's room, where tythe courts and petty sessions were once heard. The room was impressive, its main feature being a 25-feet high roof supported by a single carved kingpost.

The Red Lion was established in the 13th century as part of a monastic settlement that has gone through various stages of development since then. Perhaps its monastic beginnings are responsible for the shy and reticent spectral nun, who is very occasionally witnessed. However, in the seventies there was a spate of such sightings. I was in Kent at the time and made some enquiries at the inn after reading newspaper reports. As often happens several people knew someone who had seen the apparition but first-hand experiences were virtually non-existent.

The New Inn, Deal

To say that I was disappointed in the spirit population of Deal would be an understatement. It is not a town I know well and I have made half a dozen visits there. For a town steeped in history, smuggling and violent deaths one would have thought the place would be teeming with spirits. I was later informed that a guided walk named the 'Trail of Blood' takes place here. Researching books on the town only led me to one rather inept spirit that I do not intend to elaborate on. I could find no records of haunted pubs whatsoever.

As time was limited I tried my luck at some of the more ancient hostelries in the centre of town. I drew a blank at the first three and fared little better at the fourth, the New Inn. The young man behind the bar informed me that there were 42 pubs in town. He knew nothing about any other pub being haunted but legend dictated that the New Inn had two spirits, a good one and a bad one. He had never seen a ghost himself and did not think such things existed. However, several of his patrons had sworn to having witnessed paranormal activity on the premises. Unfortunately not one of these was in the bar at that time.

Nothing else would be gleaned here. I wandered to a placard on the wall near the inglenook. It described how the said inglenook was unknown for many years. It was not discovered until a wall was taken down during alterations. A postscript was added stating that a black cloak discovered at the time was thought to be the property of Dick Turpin.

I could not believe it!

Surely not another place for the overworked footpad to haunt.

I re-read it incredulously. Why on earth would one assume that a black cloak found in a recess was owned by Dick Turpin? The odds against are astronomical. Dick rarely strayed south of Essex or north London, but if it didn't belong to Dick who did it belong to? Possibly one of the 800,000 gentlemen of Kent who wore them at the time.

PS I once found a bowler hat in a junk shop at Portsmouth. I am convinced it belonged to Charlie Chaplin.

A story that appears in nearly every book on ghosts is the report of the phantom ship 'The Lady Lovibond'. The three-masted schooner was lost with all hands in 1748. It sank off the Goodwin Sands, north-east of Deal. Allegedly the ghost ship appears every 50 years. If you missed it in 1998 it will be along again in 2048.

A few miles north-west of Deal is the village of Eastry. It is a village steeped in myth, legend and history. One legend has it that a king of Kent murdered his two nephews here and afterwards, in a fit of conscience, he gave land for the building of Minster Abbey and Minster Church. Another legend suggests that Thomas Becket hid in some caverns carved in the chalk here. A paranormal tale comes from the 13th century church. A former vicar so loved the place that he swore he'd never leave it even after death.

Possibly his predictions came true. In 1956 a keen amateur

photographer named Bootman took a snap of the church interior. When developed the picture seems to show the former vicar, with clasped hands, knelt in prayer.

South of Deal on the Dover Road is the ruin of Oxney Court. What's left of the old place stands high above St Margaret's Bay. The apparition here is an old lady dressed in grey who crosses the main road and disappears into dense undergrowth. Several cars had reported the spectre over the years and on one occasion a bus stopped for her.

Further south is the ancient port town of Dover. A headless drummer boy that walks the walls of Dover Castle on moonlit nights was a victim of muggers during the Napoleonic wars. The boy was entrusted with the garrison's wages. To avoid being assaulted he worked his way through the labyrinth of subterranean passages below the castle. But he was ambushed, robbed and his head decapitated from his body.

Guy Underwood mentions briefly a spectral cat that frequented Dover Castle during the war. But other than the two examples mentioned above the ancient town seems surprisingly devoid of spectral beings.

The Black Robin, Kingston

Lovely old pub this, right on the bend near Black Robin Lane. The grey colour of the walls is smart rather than depressive, I was proud of myself for discovering the ghost here. It is not well-known and as far as I know it has never been reported in any other anthology.

The inside of the inn is tastefully aged and verging on the romantic. It is a gourmet's delight. Menu boards advertise mouth-watering gastronomic adventures. I well believe the manager when he tells me he's often fully booked and that people travel many miles to dine here.

So who was Black Robin?

A local highwayman, whose life-size effigy adorns the inn's lounge. As always, the figure is far too well-dressed, obviously to suit the public's misplaced conventional conception of highwaymen. Did they all really look like Errol Flynn? Or Brad Pitt to our younger readers.

Facts on Black Robin are scarce. It seems that he plied his trade on the old Dover to Canterbury Road that runs very close to the inn. Inevitably he was caught and hanged up in the hills near a cave in which he lived. I don't quite go along with this. Caught and hanged I don't doubt, but how does a man remain the ultimate picture of sartorial elegance when living in a cave? Not only that, highwaymen were always hanged in a prominent position. Firstly to assure the

God-fearing travellers that they were no longer a threat to the area and secondly to warn others against joining the profession. I would rather think that the nearby junction of the Canterbury, Dover and Folkestone Roads would have been a far more likely venue.

So does Black Robin haunt the inn?

Surprisingly not.

The tiny daughter of an ex-landlord reputedly haunts the Black Robin Inn. She was murdered up in the hills and recently her shade has been seen in the bar room.

A couple of miles north of Kingston is the attractive village of Bridge. Andrew Green *(Our Haunted Kingdom)* tells a bloodcurdling tale about the country club here. The club was once an old manor house, circa 1638.

In 1780 the owner was somewhat perplexed. His wife was returning from Scotland where she had been indisposed by illness for some years. In the interim period, the owner had been a little over familiar with a serving maid and had sired a child. His response to the situation was immediate and effective. He murdered them both. What happened to the maid's corpse is unknown but the child hid, and was slain, in the chimney. For many years sorrowful moans emanated from the said chimney.

There was also a spectral cavalier seen here several times but his story is unknown.

The White Horse, Chilham

This beautiful old Kent village has now, thankfully, been bypassed. Set at the corner of the square this is an ideal inn, in a nearly ideal setting. I say nearly ideal because the Peacock that once stood opposite has been transformed into shops, picturesque and old worldly as they may be. The haunting here is friendly and apparently nothing to do with two skeletons that were once unearthed under the kitchen floor.

I first visited the White Horse in 1967 when I read a report on the ghost that the landlord had written in the Whitbread news. I remembered well the enormous Tudor fireplace, which seemed to fill the whole room. The then time landlord was quite open and even proud of his ghost. The friendly shade of the White Horse is the Reverend Samson Hieron, vicar of Chilham in the mid 17th century. The inn was actually Hieron's home. He died in 1677 and was buried in the local churchyard. However he was not incumbent of the village at the time. Years before he had been sacked for expressing his nonconformist views.

In 1956, during some alterations, workmen opened a modern looking fireplace and discovered an inglenook behind it that was dated 1460. It is alleged that this was the beginning of the Hieron hauntings. This is a regular ghost who appears at 10:10 in the morning, not every morning of course but when he does appear it is always at that time. He is a grey-haired old man in a black gown and gaiters. He stands beside the inglenook with his hands behind his back as if warming his nether regions by the fire. Several people who have witnessed Reverend Hieron state that he is very lifelike. Apparently so much so that he has often been greeted by the observer. One customer who wished the old gentleman 'Good Day' was astonished as he turned and disappeared.

So there we have it, a benign and friendly gentlemanly ghost who apparently has been witnessed quite recently. It has been suggested that the spirit was trapped in the old fireplace and only released when workmen demolished it. I personally don't go along with this. Every ghost I ever knew could walk through walls and closed doors. Still I wonder what time the fireplace was demolished.

Could it have been 10:10 am?

Chilham Castle stands proudly on the hill within easy sight of the White Horse. The old Jacobean stronghold has the ghost of the inevitable 'grey lady'. As with many others she was reputedly walled up for some transgression or other.

Actually, early in the 20th century, some dungeons were excavated. Several skeletons were discovered, one chained to a wall. I have been unable to find out if any of them were of female gender.

South-west of Chilham, on the Ashford to Faversham Road, once stood Eastwell Park. Here a friend of Peter Underwood *(Ghosts of Kent)* related to the author a story concerning a ghostly two-wheeled barouche led by a heavily blinkered horse and driven by a man wearing a bow tie.

I had a stroll up the Pilgrims Way some years ago and remember the lake and the church mentioned in Mr Underwood's story. Not much of the church was left. The tower remains but most of it collapsed during a storm in 1951. It is thought that artillery batteries positioned here during World War II weakened the foundations.

I can remember having a distinctly uneasy feeling here.

The Ship, Dymchurch

Dymchurch, Romney Marsh country, smuggling country, home of Cephas Quested and George Ransley, contraband captains of ill repute. Dark moors and marshes, tossing seas and waylaying highwaymen. What better setting could Russell Thorndyke have had for his Doctor Syn stories.

Thorndyke's famous characters from book and screen adorn the walls of the Ship Inn. It took me back to boyish days in Saturday cinemas. The whole interior of the inn takes one tastefully back to the bloodcurdling days.

But is the Ship haunted?

I asked this question to the friendly but busy landlord.
"I have never seen anything. But there have been stories over the years."
Not much to go on and the landlord was too busy to elaborate.

I was thinking of staying here on my next visit to Kent. I informed the landlord of this and he gave me a list of prices and bedrooms. I thanked him and turned to go.
"Try and drum me up a ghost or two next time."
"No problem. You can have No 6, last week a spirit or something supernatural tore the bedclothes off a female guest."
"Are you kidding?"
"Certainly not, the sheets flew off with unbelievable force."
So there you have it, nothing else is known.

The George, Lydd

Walland Marsh is a haunting area of nothingness. It stretches from north of the A259 to Dungeness. In the winter it is particularly bleak. Gone are the heady days of the Thirties when Rollers, Bentleys and Armstrong Sidleys were loaded onto planes for the short trip to the fleshpots of Le Touquet. The village of Lydd remains, reverting to its ancient beauty. Its 130-feet church tower must have been a reassuring sight as one traversed the gaunt and desolate marshes. A stone's throw from the 'Cathedral of the Marshes' stands the George.

The George Hotel is said to be about 160 years old but I would imagine parts of it are much older. One estimate is that it goes back as far as 1420. Some type of hostelry was obviously here in smuggling times, as a fact sheet on the wall informs us that Cephas Quested and George Ransley frequented the hostelry.

The wall sheet also informs us that the inn was once run by a man with the unfortunate name of Lepper. Another landlord permitted a very brave man named Carter to hide in the building. Carter had been foolhardy enough to write and publish a pamphlet against smuggling. Affronted local smugglers surrounded the inn with cudgels and cutlasses with the intent of murdering Carter where he stood. Carter finally fled but received several severe cuts and bruises.

Undaunted but foolhardy to the point of lunacy Carter had his assailants arrested and charged in court. Not unexpectedly the poor man could find no witnesses. The charges were dropped and Carter left the area.

So who or what haunts this romantic old building?

A fiery Cephas Quested or his comrade George Ransley? A cutlass-waving crowd of smugglers perhaps? Or even the revenue men who are said to be badly wounded here? I'm afraid not. Nothing quite so exciting. The George's supernatural visitor is a ghostly cat that lands on people's beds.

Lydd is about as close as you will be able to find accommodation when visiting Wittersham. One has to cross the wilderness of Walland Marsh and the Isle of Oxney before reaching the village, which stands by the remote Rother Levels.

Andrew Green informs us the ghost of a little old lady is quite frequently seen here as she crosses the road near Poplar farmhouse. Speculation has always been rife as to whether or not this frail-looking little spectre was associated with a nearby murder some 60 years ago.

The Walnut Tree,
Aldington Corner

I approached the Walnut Tree with just the flimsiest of information about any supernatural activity there. After a lengthy interview with Karen, the young landlady, I was wondering what to leave out, how much could I cram into a couple of pages. Karen's stories were detailed, graphic and obviously sincere. But before moving on to the old inn's spectral visitors let me first do a précis on a pamphlet that gives the reader a concise history of the building.

There has been some type of dwelling on the site since Richard II's reign (1377-1399). Probably a one-roomed hut that belonged to a shepherd or fisherman.

I quote:

'A fire burned in a central hearth and an aperture in the roof, a louvre, acted as a flue.'

The pamphlet goes on to inform that later in the 15th century a small bedroom was added at a higher level that could only be reached by a ladder. Later we're told that in the 17th century beer was brewed here. Evidence for this fact is that a sales document in 1687 describes the building as a 'brewhouse'. In 1749 further documentation reveals that the building was granted a licence and registered under the name of the Walnut Tree. In the early 1800s the

Aldington gang or Aldington Blues made the village a hive of activity for smuggled goods. Either through fear, benefit or relationship the locals found it expedient to close ranks when the revenue men made enquiries. Two of the most infamous smugglers, Cephas Quested and George Ransley, made the Walnut Tree their headquarters.

The pamphlet on the inn goes on to state, 'high up on the southern side of the inn is a small window through which the gang would shine a light signalling to their confederates up on Aldington Knoll.' It also relates that as late as 1904 the inn was the venue for cockfighting contests. It further states that since this date all is above board and lawful.

When I first visited the Walnut Tree in September 2003, Karen listed some of the strange happenings. Her small son Connor had seen a man in mummy's bedroom who had given him a 'piece'. With nothing in his hand he passed the invisible 'piece' to his mother. Karen's even smaller girl, Amie, talks about another mummy. She did this whilst I was interviewing Karen. Her other mummy lives across the road and a rather complicated story involves a Mrs Chase and the doctor.

There have been reports of spectral children being seen here and psychic evenings have found the building highly informative. However the Walnut Tree's resident ghost is the above mentioned notorious George Ransley. George was finally captured and transported for life to Tasmania. Unable to return to his native Kent during his lifetime Karen believes that his ghost returned after death. George seems to have settled in quite well but is prone to fits of temper, with chairs and glasses being thrown through the air. George gets particularly upset when he thinks the family is leaving. He threw a tantrum when he saw the family packing for a holiday. In what must have been a truly bizarre scene, Karen explained to him that they would be home in a couple of weeks. This seemed to pacify George.

Other happenings worthy of note at the Walnut Tree over the years have been a body found in the well, thought to be that of an 18th century smuggler killed in a brawl, a story of bodies (casualties of the Black Death) found in a disused Mormon graveyard, a skull discovered buried in the Walnut Tree's cellar needed exorcism. From the same cellar a subterranean passage is thought to run to a church a mile away. I think that's all, other than to say that the extensions made to the building have no way diluted the internal, aged, charm of the place. The smuggling theme remains even to the words of Kipling's poem A Smugglers Song being tastefully displayed on the wall. I am told that the liquor and vitals are excellent.

PS I nearly forgot. A Communion is practised here on some Wednesday nights.

A couple of miles to the south-west in the village of Bilsington a ruined abbey has a strange story. The Priory, once owned by politician Sir William Cosway, (a massive obelisk venerates the forgotten man), is said to be haunted by Augustian monks. Mrs Conrad, wife of author Joseph Conrad, was one such witness.

Slightly to the south-east of Aldington stands the famous Lympne Castle. A Roman guard who accidentally fell to his death from the high walls is thought to the responsible for footsteps heard mounting an ancient tower. Six Saxons, thought to have been slaughtered by Normans, also haunt the old building and a figure in Tudor attire has been witnessed.

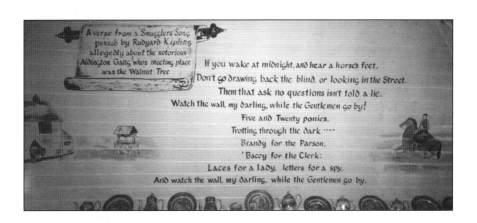

Sir William Harvey,
Willesborough

Wonderful old pub this but unfortunately not open when I visited. It is a pity that so much housing has been inflicted on this attractive village. It is not difficult to imagine this winding road as it once might have been many years ago, before the M20 slashed its way across the Kent countryside.

Sir William Harvey, as we all know, was the 17th century physician who discovered that blood flowed from the heart in the arterial system and back towards the heart in the veinous system. He published his findings in the *Movement of the Heart* (1628). It is nice to see that the old chap has been honoured by a local hospital. Sir William does not haunt the inn bearing his name. I am afraid that the phantom here is yet another spectral coach and horses. The rather tenuous connection is that on various occasions the ghostly stagecoach has been seen, or heard, from the inn's front door. There is a story of there being an underground passage between the inn

and Boys Hall, a couple of hundred yards away. Legend states Charles II used the tunnel whilst he was in hiding. However, there have been no reports of any ghostly apparitions of this royal gentleman.

Boys Hall has ghosts and also a plethora of mysteriously romantic tales concerning murder, betrayal and supernatural encounters. Andrew Green in his *Our Haunted Kingdom* tells a fascinating story. But as it is Mr Green's tale and this book is dedicated to haunted inns, with just the most fleeting references to other strange happenings, I shall say no more.

Kent publicans have a rather easygoing attitude to opening time. They lack the sense of urgency of their colleagues in my native Berkshire. This being the case I took the opportunity of at least a look at Boys Hall. There is a high, stout wall, which makes the old house impossible to see from the road. The only glimpse one can obtain from the main road is as it rises over the motorway. From what I could see the house has retained its mysterious, almost awesome, countenance. On my return I passed a gate proudly announcing Little Boys Hall. My colleague just had to say it.

"At least we know where the little boys' room is."

Why have I no refined friends?

The Duke's Head, Sellindge

Here is another old inn with the most tenuous of ghostly associations. The hostelry stands beside the old A20, Folkestone to London Road, and was once a paradise for highwaymen. If one can imagine the area thick with bushes it makes a story a little more plausible.

I shall tell it as I heard it.

Two highwaymen frequented the Duke's Head in the late 18th century. The alehouse (probably rejoicing in another name in those days) was a short distance from the men's cottage. The highwaymen rented a large barn from the landlord. The barn lay some way off the road and could only be approached by a bridleway that ran through the thicket alongside the inn.

For some unknown reason the highwaymen left their horses in the barn one night whilst they sprang out on a passing stage. The venue for their last hold-up was a nearby bend in the road that was overhung by long branches. It was a popular place for robbing coaches. So popular in fact that the authorities had set a trap. As our heroes leapt down from the overhanging branches half a dozen pistols were aimed at them. Arrested, they were taken to Ashford and later hanged at Tonbridge. What is mystifying is that the men didn't inform the authorities of where to find their horses. The poor animals starved to death. A possible answer to this is that they were hoping for an eleventh hour reprieve, which never materialised. Or possibly there was a valuable cache hidden in the barn.

The ghostly footsteps and heavy breathing that is/was sometimes heard beside the Duke's Head has been interpreted as the frantic highwaymen rushing to save their steeds.

An unlikely story? I suppose it is but I have told it as I heard it. Enough said.

The Bell, Hythe

I cannot believe that previous writers on the supernatural found no haunted pubs in Canterbury, Deal or Hythe. I have not read of one such entry in my numerous ghost books. However, what is to follow must be the shortest report and interview ever.

I pulled into the Bell on a Saturday lunchtime. The landlord seemed jovial and good-natured. The inn is reputedly the oldest in Hythe. The available information gave me a chance to broach a brief conversation with mine host.

"Is this the oldest pub in Hythe?" I enquired.

"They say it is, parts of it go back to the 15th century."

"A building that old should have a resident ghost."

"I've heard tell we have a ghostly lady in the cellar."

"A grey lady?"

"That's right. How did you know?"

"They all are. Have you ever seen her?"

"No never and I've been here five years."

"Who has seen her?"

"A few of my older customers."

"Any in here now?"

"No I am afraid not."

It was a good pint of bitter anyway.

Incidentally, did anyone know that St Leonard's church at Hythe has hundreds of skulls and skeletons stacked up in it? Unfortunately I didn't find this out until I was back home in Berkshire.

The King's Head, Hythe

This is another ancient and lively pub. I happened to visit on the nearest weekend to March 17 and the landlord was celebrating St Patrick's Day with some flair and joviality. I made my way between leprechauns, dancers, an Irish karaoke and a couple of dozen massive green hats. Realising that it would be pointless inquiring anything of the landlord until things quietened down I ordered a steak. When it was delivered I was told that it would be the last one that evening as the oven had caught fire. When I finally got to talk to the landlord he asked me if I had read about his hauntings in the newspaper or seen reports on the television. I replied in the negative to both questions. I had heard nothing but travelling around Kent and calling on literally hundreds of pubs I thought this one to be old enough to be of interest. It was fairly general stuff, lights turning on and off, beer pumps being affected and doors opening and closing.

I enquired if the doors had not been blown open.

"Certainly not," he replied.

He went on to point out that his small daughter had often experienced the door incidents and had called him as witness on several occasions.

"I closed the door, but it immediately opened again," he said.

"You're certain it was not a draft?"

"I have never seen a draft that can turn a door handle," he replied.

There is little more to say.

The Clarendon, Sandgate

I stayed overnight in the Hythe area at Sandgate. Just up the hill, a short but precipitous one, stands the Clarendon. I called in during the afternoon and again in the evening. I made a casual remark about the steep hill and another about the age of the hostelry. From there the landlady and I spoke of her in-house ghost.

"It is a thrower," she explained. "Things jump out of cupboards at you, tea cloths, saucers, soup tins etc. We had a dish that shot out of the microwave, fluttered in mid-air then crashed to the floor."

"Have you witnessed anything else?"

"Yes, suicidal glasses. Pint mugs that stand on the back of a shelf suddenly leap two feet forward with lemming-like suicidal intent."

I suggested that the steep angle of the hill I had just conquered might have something to do with this, but the landlady would have none of it.

"These articles don't slide, they are propelled with some force," she replied. "My husband opened a cupboard door once and a hurricane force wind rushed out past him."

There was little else to say, except that the bitter was very good.

Whilst in this neck of the woods there are several other places that might entice the ghost hunter's interest.

A mile or two north-west of Hythe stands the village of Saltwood. Here a road passes from the village to Sandling Station. Near to where it passes Slaybrook farm a strange flickering light has been seen. As it approaches it becomes a burning ball and transforms into a man carrying a lamp. There also a ghostly Roman soldier, thought to have been slain and robbed; a Victorian landowner and one of the murderers of Thomas Becket.

Several miles east of Saltwood lies Cheriton, virtually part of Folkestone in everything other the name. Here, Underhill House has experienced at least one murder and three suicides. The old house was utilised by the army for many years. Peter Underwood (*Ghosts of*

Kent) informs us that an army officer plagued by debts shot himself here. An officer's batman fatally slit his girlfriend's throat and before he could be arrested shot himself. Also, for reasons unknown, an army padre hanged himself.

The offending spirits seem to be a young soldier, an old man in a pepper and salt suit and a playful poltergeist.

In Folkestone itself at the Bayle, ghostly monks have been seen and heard, and at Leas Pavilion, actors and stagehands have had the feeling of being watched. I always take this sort of report with a pinch of salt. It's a feeling we've all had from time to time, no matter what our surroundings.

So good reader here ends my ghostly pub crawl of Kent. Over 600 pubs were actually visited by my good self in the county. Of the 50 or so reported 25 (50%) have never come to light in any other ghost book. I should know, I have hundreds. The other 75 briefly mentioned spooks are tolerably well known; therefore I've only made the briefest of references. I hope once more that the reader enjoys perusing them as much as I enjoyed researching them, and of course it's a lot cheaper for the reader.

"One for the road Rog?"

"Don't mind if I do," let's try the Water's Edge at Hythe.

The Water's Edge,
(ex Red Lion), Hythe

Once again this is a contestant for the oldest pub in Hythe. It was late Saturday night when I called in, I had made six calls at lunchtime and this was the eighth that evening. The pub was extremely busy but I finally got around to talking to the landlord whilst I ordered refreshment.

"I've heard this old pub is haunted," I lied.

"I've never seen anything but you should talk to Liz," he replied as he nodded towards a young, attractive and extremely busy barmaid.

I finally got to talk to Liz and asked if she had experienced anything inexplicable here.

"We have got a ghost called Albert," she replied rather coyly. "But I'm not going to talk about it if you're going to take the p***."

I quickly informed Liz that that was not my intention. Having convinced her I was in earnest I received the following information.

Albert was a tram driver during the war. Unfortunately his tram was hit by masonry following a bomb raid. He was carried into the pub where he died shortly after. Here Liz pointed to a photograph on the wall. I assumed it was a picture of a crushed tram. However the sheen on the glass made it impossible to photograph and a hearty crowd drinking underneath it made it nigh impossible to reach. Liz went on to state that she had seen Albert on several occasions. He wore blue overalls, a uniform jacket and a dated flat and peaked cap. The ghostly tram driver indulged in a mild form of poltergeist activity. Chairs had been pulled out from under tables, glasses shattered with no one near them, light bulbs followed their example, exploding regularly, and Christmas decorations fell and occasionally caught alight.

"Was there anything more ambitious?" I asked.

"Can you see that large advert on the wall by the door?"

I nodded in the affirmative, looking at a large barrel top that had been painted. I guessed it weighed between 15 and 20 pounds.

"That fell to the floor, but it was held in place by three large bolts."

Liz went on to say that she had heard strange voices and sobbing. Could this be Albert's lamenting relatives?

Having sufficient evidence for an entry in this book I returned to my company and Liz returned to her work. About 10 minutes later I felt a tap on the shoulder. Liz presented me with glass that had been neatly dissected without breaking. The tumbler lay in two perfect halves. To make the description plainer the top half had been removed symmetrically from the bottom half and both rims were absolutely smooth.

"A bit of Albert's work?" I shouted above the crowd.

"That's right," she replied.

In hindsight I should have ascertained when the glass had been dissected.

I shall return.